On the "Meaning" of Politics

This book offers a concise, yet provocative, summation of Christos Yannaras' long reflection on the meaning of politics. It provides vital clarification on Yannaras' conception and understanding of politics and his interpretation of its historical development in the Western and Eastern theological/civilizational traditions. The book critiques the Western (Christian) tradition of political thought and praxis, namely its individualistic epistemology, its utilitarian political organization, its obsession with rationalistic efficiency, and its religionized Christianity with all the destructive ideologies flowing therefrom. It aims to recover and counterpose a Greco-Christian conception and practice of politics based on communion, the *ecclesia*, truth as a collective and common contest or struggle to discover, reveal and manifest cosmic reality and an ontological vision of humans living in harmony with the ornamental order of the universe. With a foreword by Rowan Williams, this is a highly original and significant meditation on the meaning of politics that will be of interest to both political theologians and political philosophers.

Christos Yannaras is Professor Emeritus at Panteion University of Social and Political Sciences in Athens, Greece.

Jonathan Cole is Assistant Director of the Centre for Religion, Ethics and Society at Charles Sturt University in Canberra, Australia.

Transforming Political Theologies
Series Editors: Judith Gruber, Vincent Lloyd and David True

Titles in the series include

Witnessing Peace
Becoming Agents Under Duress in Colombia
Janna L. Hunter-Bowman

On the "Meaning" of Politics
Christos Yannaras
Translated to English by Jonathan Cole

For more information about this series, please visit: www.routledge.com/Transforming-Political-Theologies/book-series/TRPT

On the "Meaning" of Politics

Christos Yannaras

Translated to English by Jonathan Cole

LONDON AND NEW YORK

First published 2024
by Routledge
4 Park Square, Milton Park, Abingdon, Oxon OX14 4RN

and by Routledge
605 Third Avenue, New York, NY 10158

Routledge is an imprint of the Taylor & Francis Group, an informa business

© 2024 Christos Yannaras, translated to English by Jonathan Cole

The right of Christos Yannaras and Jonathan Cole to be identified as authors of this work has been asserted in accordance with sections 77 and 78 of the Copyright, Designs and Patents Act 1988.

All rights reserved. No part of this book may be reprinted or reproduced or utilised in any form or by any electronic, mechanical, or other means, now known or hereafter invented, including photocopying and recording, or in any information storage or retrieval system, without permission in writing from the publishers.

Trademark notice: Product or corporate names may be trademarks or registered trademarks, and are used only for identification and explanation without intent to infringe.

British Library Cataloguing-in-Publication Data
A catalogue record for this book is available from the British Library

ISBN: 978-1-032-49314-5 (hbk)
ISBN: 978-1-032-53207-3 (pbk)
ISBN: 978-1-003-41086-7 (ebk)

DOI: 10.4324/9781003410867

Typeset in Times New Roman
by Apex CoVantage, LLC

Contents

Foreword vii
Translator's note ix
Translator's acknowledgements x

Introduction 1

1 Reverence and justice 13
2 Necessity and freedom 15
3 Forms of organized coexistence 17
4 Cohesion through coercion 19
5 *Leitourgima*'s degeneration into office 21
6 *Ratio* dethrones authority 23
7 The desire for "salvation" dethrones *ratio* 25
8 *Ecclesia* and religion: incompatible modes of existence 26
9 When truth becomes the priority 28
10 Politics: contest or art? 32
11 Shared need as shared truth 35

12	The pre-political character of freedom	38
13	The alignment of the *ecclesia* of the demos and the *ecclesia* of the believers	40
14	The exercise of authority as responsible service	43
15	The common roots of democracy, community, and the parish	46
16	The political consequences of the *Ecclesia*'s religionization	48
17	Religious totalitarianism	50
18	Ideology: the alienation of truth into accuracy	52
19	*Societas*: the alienation of communion into partnership	54
20	Religious "salvation" and political individualism	57
21	Materialistic and idealistic utilitarianism	60
22	The *Ecclesia* is the aim of politics	63
23	Augustine is Europe	67
24	Political forms of religious individualism	70
25	The *Ecclesia*'s alienation in confessionalism	72
26	A Trinitarian archetype of politics	74
27	Comprehension is not knowledge	76
	Bibliography	*78*
	Index	*81*

Foreword

Christos Yannaras can always be relied upon to overturn the Western reader's intellectual assumptions, and this intensely illuminating and challenging little essay is no exception. Most of what we take for granted about the relation of faith and politics is dismantled here; we are told that all true political activity is actually in search of the reality found in the church; we are warned about the Western habit of imagining knowledge to be the management of objects whose passive shapes we can define and manipulate; and much more. Yannaras has often insisted that the fundamental error of the civilization of the West is to suppose that Christianity is a religion, when in fact it is the embodied reality of *communion*; and politics is essentially to do with communion—not with supplementing individual problem-solving with collective problem-solving, clubbing together to be more efficient, as rather too many political philosophies assume.

The political, as definitively conceived in classical Greek thinking, is to do with true knowing. This is something wholly distinct from acquiring a large amount of accurate information; it is living in alignment with reality, living in a way that is in touch with, and open to, eternal life. Truth is the state of life which is delivered from the death of individualism—the fatal myth that we are self-sufficient and that the meanings we discover are only the formations of private speculative thought. Historically, for all sorts of reasons, Christianity has been lured into one or another version of the false equation of truth with accurate information and with the myth of the human subject as fundamentally the possessor of information. The church has been deformed into a machinery that guarantees true information—and imposes it by force. And so when that oppressive and unjust force is resisted, a new and opposite error arises: instead of a truth enforced, we have a truth interiorized and a concept of law as simply the control of potentially violent diversity between individuals and self-interested groups.

The task is to rediscover the ontological sense of truth, and this entails a radical re-thinking of politics. Life together, life in communion, is life in which we are implicated all the time in meeting human needs together, the needs that have to do with our grounding in freedom and love and our growth into fullness of life. This is not a policy that follows on from some carefully reasoned survey of what appear to be necessities for human survival; it is a recognition that our interconnectedness is far deeper than we know. The church is the environment in which that interconnectedness is most completely clear and most radically activated, as we are fed together in the Eucharistic meal. This is the ultimate political fact, the place where the *polis* is manifested and renewed. The church's tragedy is to have lost sight of this almost completely—certainly in the world of Western Christianity—becoming an ideological society that dissolves the Eucharistic gift of life into an abstract moralism and an obsession with correct teaching, bowing down to the idols of an infallible scripture or an infallible pontiff—or indeed an infallible rational modernity.

Yannaras does not offer a manifesto for some sort of integrist Christian politics. He poses a far deeper set of questions about how we see our personal reality, what we mean by knowledge and whether we are at all interested any longer in living truthfully, living in contact and alignment with the real. He takes no prisoners; many readers will want to protest at a good many points and argue that Augustine or Newman or Bonhoeffer might prove far more of an ally than Yannaras allows. But it is important to allow the comprehensiveness of his challenge to sink in. Not least, it is important that a contemporary Western church much preoccupied with its public profile and recruitment should stop and ask whether it is not slipping ever more completely into the mold of the religious ideology that Yannaras so comprehensively critiques. If it is at times a difficult work, the difficulty is not with abstruse language or abstract concepts but with the sheer scale of the imaginative change of heart required to make sense of it. It is a wonderfully concentrated digest of some of the most innovative thinking of one of Europe's most original, passionate, and visionary theologians, and it is a great gift to have this lucid and careful translation.

Rowan Williams
Cardiff, July 2021

Translator's note

Yannaras routinely emphasizes the etymology of Greek terms in ways that are impossible to replicate in English. He does so by inserting non-standard hyphens between the constituent parts of compound Greek terms. This presents his translator with a unique challenge. Wherever possible, I have drawn attention to these etymological emphases and allusions in footnotes, explaining both the typical Modern Greek meaning of the word and the etymological meaning highlighted by Yannaras.

The Greek text is written in a clipped style that might strike the native English speaker as abrupt. I have taken the liberty of adding English connectors and the occasional word that is not found in the Greek original to help conform the translation to the conventions of English prose. On occasion I have been forced to employ a somewhat free translation in order to render the meaning of Yannaras' unique Greek prose intelligible to a native English speaker. This has all been done in the name of making the English translation read as smoothly as possible for the native English speaker, while faithfully capturing the sense of the original text.

For the most part, I have relied on existing translations of classical Greek, Patristic, and biblical texts cited by Yannaras, making adaptations where Yannaras' reading explicitly departs from the translation used, or where it is clear from context that Yannaras uses or reads vocabulary from the text in a way that differs from the translation used. Where no existing English translation is credited, the translation is my own.

Translator's acknowledgements

I thank Sotiris Mitralexis for reviewing the fidelity of the translation and making valuable suggestions for improvement that were incorporated into the final manuscript. I also thank Wayne Hudson and Simon Kennedy for reading the manuscript and providing feedback on its readability from the point of view of English speakers unfamiliar with the Greek original. A special and heartfelt thanks goes to Christos Yannaras for graciously responding to my requests for clarification regarding the meaning of the Greek text. Lastly, and in no way least of all, I acknowledge a special debt of gratitude to Dimitris Panagopoulos for his generous financial support that made this project possible. His ongoing commitment to the translation of Yannaras' corpus is a gift to scholarship.

Introduction

Jonathan Cole

On the "Meaning" of Politics serves as a succinct, yet culminating, statement of Christos Yannaras' political thought. The "intensely illuminating and demanding" essay, as Rowan Williams aptly describes it in his foreword, published in Greek in Yannaras' eighty-fourth year, is the product of a lifetime of reflection on the meaning of existence, and in particular that most significant and consequential expression of human existence we have come to know by the name "politics"—the collective human life of the *polis*.

The present work forms part of an informal series of recent, shorter books summarizing and revisiting questions and themes pursued throughout Yannaras' prolific career. Aside from *On the "Meaning" of Politics*, published in Greek in 2019, the series includes the following untranslated works: *An Ontology of Personhood (A Person-Centered Ontology)*[i] and *Here and Beyond (An Attempt at Ontological Interpretation)*,[ii] both in 2016; *Fall, Judgment, and Hell—Or the Way that Legalistic Thinking Undermines Ontology*, in 2017;[iii] and *Homage to Nietzsche*, in 2020.[iv]

On the "Meaning" of Politics synthesizes ideas relating to politics, history, culture, and epistemology articulated across substantive works like *Rationalism and Social Practice* (1984, untranslated),[v] *The Inhumanity of Right* (1998; translated),[vi] and *Reality and Illusion in Political Economy* (2006, untranslated),[vii] as well as thousands of articles published in Greek

---

i Christos Yannaras, Ὀντολογία τοῦ προσώπου (προσωποκεντρικὴ ὀντολογία) [*An Ontology of Personhood (A Person-Centered Ontology)*] (Athens: Ikaros, 2016).
ii Christos Yannaras, Ἐνθάδε—Ἐπέκεινα (ἀπόπειρες ὀντολογικῆς ἑρμηνευτικῆς) [*Here and Beyond (An Attempt at Ontological Interpretation)*] (Athens: Ikaros, 2016).
iii Christos Yannaras, Πτώση, Κρίση, Κόλαση ἢ δικανικὴ ὑπονόμευση τῆς ὀντολογίας [*Fall, Judgment and Hell: Or the Way That Legalistic Thinking Undermines Ontology* (Athens: Ikaros, 2017).
iv Christos Yannaras, Ἀντιχάρισμα στὸν Νίτσε [*Homage to Nietzsche*] (Athens: Ikaros, 2020).
v Christos Yannaras, Ὀρθὸς λόγος καὶ κοινωνικὴ πρακτική [*Rationalism and Social Practice*] (Athens: Domos, 1984).
vi Christos Yannaras, Ἡ ἀπανθρωπία τοῦ δικαιώματος (Athens: Domos, 1998); Christos Yannaras, *The Inhumanity of Right*, trans. Norman Russell (Cambridge: James Clarke & Co, 2021).
vii Christos Yannaras, Τὸ πραγματικὸ καὶ τὸ φαντασιῶδες στὴν Πολιτικὴ Οἰκονομία [*Reality and Illusion in Political Economy*] (Athens: Domos, 2006).

DOI: 10.4324/9781003410867-1

2 Introduction

newspapers since the 1960s. Many of these articles have been published in volumes—an incredible 39, to be precise, all of them untranslated.[viii] Remarkably, at the time of writing this introduction, Yannaras, now eighty-seven years of age, is still producing a weekly column published in *Kathimerini*. Cataloging, examining, and assessing Yannaras' voluminous and untranslated newspaper columns, which true to style offer a more philosophical analysis of Greek and global politics than is typically found in newspapers, remains a vital, yet daunting, task for future scholarship.

Yannaras is a provocative and controversial thinker. His oeuvre has accordingly generated a contested reception, both within and outside Greece, and evinces all the hallmarks of remaining contested well into the future. This will likely increase as interest in his thought beyond Greece, and outside the Eastern Orthodox theological tradition, continues to grow. In this regard, it is worth highlighting two problematics born of Yannaras' Greek context and experience that have long animated his political thought, and which will help to illuminate *On the "Meaning" of Politics*. They might also serve to

---

viii In order of original publication year, but with details for current editions: Christos Yannaras, *Ἡ κρίση τῆς προφητείας* [*Prophetic Judgment*] 4th ed. (Athens: Ikaros, 2010); Christos Yannaras, *Τὸ προνόμιο τῆς ἀπελπισίας* [*The Prerogative of Despair*] 2nd ed. (Athens: Grigoris, 1973); Christos Yannaras, *Κεφάλαια Πολιτικῆς Θεολογίας* [*Chapters in Political Theology*] 3rd ed. (Athens: Grigoris, 1983); Christos Yannaras, *Ἡ Νεοελληνικὴ Ταυτότητα* [*Neo-Hellenic Identity*] 4th ed. (Athens: Grigoris, 2001); Christos Yannaras, *Κριτικὲς παρεμβάσεις* [*Critical Interventions*] 4th ed. (Athens: Domos, 1993); Christos Yannaras, *Τὸ κενὸ στὴν τρέχουσα πολιτική* [*The Void in Contemporary Politics*] 2nd ed. (Athens: Kastaniotis, 1992); Christos Yannaras, *Ἑλλαδικὰ προτελεύτια* [*The End of the Greek State*] 2nd ed. (Athens: Kastaniotis, 1992); Christos Yannaras, *Πολιτικὴ χρονογραφία 1: Χώρα ὑποχείρια παιγνίου* [*Political Chronicles Part 1: A Country That Is a Pawn in a Game*] (Athens: Kastaniotis, 1994); Christos Yannaras, *Πολιτικὴ χρονογραφία 2: Ἀπερισκέπτως αὐτόχειρες* [*Political Chronicles Part 2: Rushing to Suicide*] (Athens: Kastaniotis, 1994); Christos Yannaras, *Πολιτικὴ χρονογραφία 3: Κύκλος φαῦλος στροβιλώδης* [*Political Chronicles Part 3: A Turbulent Vicious Circle*] (Athens: Kastaniotis, 1994); Christos Yannaras, *Ἀφελληνισμοῦ παρεπόμενα* [*The Consequences of De-Hellenization*] 2nd ed. (Athens: Kaktos, 2005); Christos Yannaras, *Ἑλληνότροπος πολιτική* [*The Greek Style of Politics*] (Athens: Ikaros, 1996); Christos Yannaras, *Ἀντιστάσεις στὴν ἀλλοτρίωση* [*Resisting Alienation*] 2nd ed. (Athens: Ikaros, 2008); Christos Yannaras, *Πολιτισμός, τὸ κεντρικὸ πρόβλημα τῆς πολιτικῆς* [*Culture: The Central Problem of Politics*] 2nd ed. (Athens: Kaktos, 2005); Christos Yannaras, *Ἰχνηλασία νοήματος* [*Outline of Meaning*] (Athens: Livanis, 1998); Christos Yannaras, *Ἡ παρακμὴ ὡς πρόκληση* [*Decline as Provocation*] (Athens: Livanis, 2000); Christos Yannaras, *Ἑλληνικὴ ἑτοιμότητα γιὰ τὴν εὐρωπαϊκὴ ἑνοποίηση* [*Is Greece Ready for Union with Europe?*] (Athens: Livanis, 2000); Christos Yannaras, *Παιδεία καὶ γλῶσσα* [*Education and Language*] 5th ed. (Athens: Patakis, 2003); Christos Yannaras, *Ἡ Ἀριστερὰ ὡς Δεξιὰ—Ἡ Δεξιὰ ὡς παντομίμα* [*The Left as Right: The Right as Pantomime*] 2nd ed. (Athens: Patakis, 2001); Christos Yannaras, *Κομματοκρατία* [*Rule by Parties*] 3rd ed. (Athens: Patakis, 2004); Christos Yannaras, *Εἰς μικρὸν γενναῖοι—Ὁδηγίες χρήσεως* [*A Guide to Being Brave against the Odds*] (Athens: Patakis, 2003); Christos Yannaras, *Προφορικὴ ἀμεσότητα* [*Verbal Immanence*] 2nd ed. (Thessaloniki: Ianos, 2003); Christos Yannaras, *Ἡ λογικὴ ἀρχίζει μὲ τὸν ἔρωτα* [*Logic Begins with Love*] 2nd ed. (Athens: Ikaros, 2007); Christos Yannaras, *Κοινωνιοκεντρικὴ Πολιτική: Κριτήρια* [*Criteria for a Communion-Centered Politics*] (Athens:

Introduction 3

ameliorate common misunderstandings of his approach. These are the related problematics of Greek identity and Greek political dysfunction.

The problematic of Greek identity relates to the fractured nature of contemporary Greek culture, underlaid, as it is, by a uniquely complex, variegated, and contested historical legacy—the philosophy of ancient Greek city-state ecology, the Christian theology of the Greek fathers, the Christian civilization of Byzantium, four centuries of Ottoman colonization, the emergence of a modern Greek nation-state modeled on Western European constitutional forms, and eventual integration into the European Union. The problematic of Greek political dysfunction relates to the fractious, often unstable, and turbulent political history of the modern Greek nation-state since its first partial independence in 1832.[ix]

The unsuccessful amalgam of Eastern and Western influences in contemporary Greek culture, religion, and politics, as Yannaras' diagnoses it, has left Greeks in a state of cultural "schizophrenia" and with a dysfunctional politics. Yannaras' strident and vigorous critique of what he regards to be pernicious Western influences that have corrupted Greece's Eastern Orthodox faith and spirituality, and bequeathed its political life with alien and stillborn political institutions, namely, individualism, consumerism, materialism, rationalism, ideology, legalism and more, have often been misread as a form of Eastern Orthodox chauvinism and, for Greek critics, as being uncomfortably close to the orbit of right-wing Greek nationalism. But this misunderstands both the motivations and location of Yannaras' political

---

Estias, 2007); Christos Yannaras, Μαχόμενη ἀνελπιστία [Fighting the Unexpected] 2nd ed. (Athens: Estias, 2005); Christos Yannaras, Ἔπαινος ψήφου τιμωρητικῆς [In Praise of a Protest Vote] 2nd ed. (Thessaloniki: Ianos, 2008); Christos Yannaras, Ἡ κατάρρευση τοῦ πολιτικοῦ συστήματος στὴν Ἑλλάδα σήμερα [The Collapse of the Political System in Greece Today] 2nd ed. (Thessaloniki: Ianos, 2010); Christos Yannaras, Τὸ πολιτικὸ ζητούμενο στὴν Ἑλλάδα σήμερα [The Political Challenge in Greece Today] 2nd ed. (Thessaloniki: Ianos, 2010); Christos Yannaras, Κατὰ κεφαλὴν καλλιέργεια [Per Capita Cultivation] 2nd ed. (Thessaloniki: Ianos, 2011); Christos Yannaras, Ἡ πολιτικὴ γονιμότητα τῆς ὀργῆς [The Fertile Politics of Anger] (Thessaloniki: Ianos, 2011); Christos Yannaras, Τὸ πρόβλημά μας εἶναι πολιτικό, ὄχι οἰκονομικό [Our Problem is Political, Not Economic] (Thessaloniki: Ianos, 2013); Christos Yannaras, Ἡ ἑλληνικότητα ὡς ποιότητα καὶ ὡς ντροπή [Greek Identity as Quality and Shame] (Thessaloniki: Ianos, 2014); Christos Yannaras, Finis Graeciae (Thessaloniki: Ianos, 2014); Christos Yannaras, Τόπος τοῦ ἀνοίκειου τρόπου [In an Unfamiliar Mode] (Thessaloniki: Ianos, 2015); Christos Yannaras, Τὴν ἀλήθεια κατάματα [Staring Truth in the Face] (Thessaloniki: Ianos, 2016); Christos Yannaras, Νὰ ἐπαναστατήσει ἡ ἀξιοπρέπεια [Self-Respect Demands Revolt] (Thessaloniki: Ianos, 2017); Christos Yannaras, Ἑλληνοκεντρικὸς ἐκσυγχρονισμός [Greek-centric Modernization] (Thessaloniki: Ianos, 2018); Christos Yannaras, Ἀντιπαλεύοντας τὸ πολιτικὸ τίποτα [Resisting Political Nihilism] (Thessaloniki: Ianos, 2019).

ix The Greek uprising against Ottoman rule began in 1821, had succeeded in creating a de facto autonomous Greek state by 1827, but only attained international recognition in 1832. Greece's sovereign borders subsequently expanded in an iterative fashion reaching final form in 1946 with the acquisition of the Dodecanese Islands from Italy.

critique. In the first instance, it fails to take into account the aforementioned animating problematics that stimulate Yannaras' work: Greek identity and political dysfunction, both of which are existential, not abstract, questions for Yannaras. It is not Greek nationalistic superiority, nor Orthodox sectarianism, that have impelled Yannaras' critique of the Western intellectual tradition, as well as its political and cultural products. It is their failure in the Greek context, which is to say in Yannaras' own lived experience. It is this experience that drove him to the conclusion that Western civilization is a corrosive and corrupting influence on account of its moral, cultural, and spiritual bankruptcy. While the civilizational scope of Yannaras' critique will undoubtedly strike some readers as too expansive, unbridled, and unqualified, such a critique is becoming more, not less, resonant with critiques now routinely encountered by thinkers living in Western liberal democracies, particularly in the English-speaking world.[x]

In some ways, Yannaras is a victim of losing faith in liberalism decades before such a loss of faith became common among English-speaking intellectuals who inhabit polities that have only more recently come to appear brittle, tired, degenerate, and dysfunctional. Yannaras is also a victim of the emergence of Orthodox reformist movements dedicated to a project of integrating the fruits of liberalism into an Orthodox worldview, namely care and concern for minorities, respect for human rights, and the embrace of pluralism. Yannaras' critique of the West, including its dominant liberal ideological scaffolding, has come to be seen as an obstacle to progress in reformist circles dedicated to dragging the Orthodox Church out of its perceived ethno-tribal pathologies. This is ironic given more and more Catholic and Protestant intellectuals are embracing a postliberal perspective that has synergy with Yannaras' critique of Western political ideas and practices.

As Yannaras has made explicit in his writing, his critique of the West is immanent. He was born into a Western nation-state, society, and culture, educated in a Western intellectual tradition (with postgraduate study in both Germany and France), and reared in a Western spirituality (see below). "My entire work and life," he wrote in 2013,

> has been a dialogue with my Western self, a search, in my Greek ecclesial roots, for serious (experientially shared) answers to the problems of the modern West, which is the flesh of my day-to-day life.[xi]

The turbulent political era that spans Yannaras' lifetime in Greece, beginning in 1935, has made him witness to some of the worst excesses of the Western

---

[x] See, for example, John Milbank and Adrian Pabst, *The Politics of Virtue: Post-Liberalism and the Human Future* (London: Rowman & Littlefield, 2016).
[xi] Yannaras, Ἡ ἑλληνικότητα ὡς ποιότητα καὶ ὡς ντροπή, 300.

Introduction 5

political tradition. Among Yannaras' earliest memories, recounted in his untranslated autobiography, *Refuge of Ideas*, is the Nazi occupation of Greece (he watched the German forces enter the city from his rooftop terrace as a young boy), and, in particular, the devastating famine that ensued in Athens as a consequence.[xii] It is easy to overlook the fact that Yannaras spent the first years of his life under fascist regimes, initially that of Greek dictator Ioannis Metaxas, immediately followed by those of foreign fascists—Germany, Italy, and Bulgaria each administered part of Greece during the Axis occupation— aided by Greek collaborators. Civil war ensued (1944–1949), as communist partisans and royalists backed by the United Kingdom vied for control of liberated Greece. It goes without saying that neither fascism nor communism are products of the theology, spirituality, and history of Eastern Orthodox Christianity, or the political philosophy and practices of the ancient Greek *polis*.

Yannaras has experienced the full variety of Western political ideologies, institutions, and modes of organization. In addition to the violence of fascism and communism, he has experienced republicanism, constitutional monarchy, liberalism, social democracy, military dictatorship, nationalism, and, more recently, the ruthless application of bitter neoliberal medicine to a bankrupt state at the hands of a set of international institutions—the European Union, International Monetary Fund, and European Central Bank—most of which, again, cannot claim any genuine spiritual or intellectual origin in either classical Greek political philosophy or Eastern Orthodox theology.

It is also important to understand that Yannaras' initial theological and spiritual formation occurred inside the *Zoe* brotherhood, a para-ecclesial organization intent on reviving Christianity in Greece, with a Protestant-like (fundamentalist) spiritual ethos, with its missionary zeal, emphasis on moral purity, separatist tendencies, and obsession with doctrinal conformity. Indeed, Yannaras has quipped that *Zoe* outdid even Greek communists in terms of conspiratorial organization and structure, as well as the policing of members.[xiii] Yannaras was catechized into *Zoe* at a young age and remained enmeshed in the movement into adulthood. *Zoe*, in Yannaras' experience, proved to be yet another instance of Greece's intellectual and spiritual colonization by the West, following liberation from Ottoman rule. Yannaras eventually left *Zoe* and embarked on a theological journey that would see him become one of the leading figures in Greek theology's rediscovery and reclamation of its Orthodox patrimony, a member of the famed "generation of the 1960s" in Greek theology.[xiv]

---

xii Christos Yannaras, Καταφύγιο Ἰδεῶν [*Refuge of Ideas*] 8th ed. (Athens: Ikaros, 2011), 12–13. Yannaras recounts seeing local officials loading the corpses of the deceased from starvation onto carts in the streets of Athens during this period.
xiii Ibid., 36–7.
xiv For an overview of the development of Greek theology in the twentieth century and the role of the "generation of the 1960s," see Pantelis Kalaitzidis, "New Trends in Greek Orthodox Theology: Challenges in the Movement towards a Genuine Renewal and Christian Unity," *Scottish Journal of Theology* 67, no. 2 (2014): 127–64.

6 Introduction

This theological turn has not been without its controversy, and Yannaras has had a rather fractious and difficult relationship with the theological establishment in Greece. His first attempt at a PhD in theology met with disappointment. The thesis, submitted to the School of Theology at the National Kapodistrian University of Athens, following three years of postgraduate study in Germany, elicited a hostile reception that led to an impasse over demands for wholesale revisions which Yannaras' conscience did not enable him to make. The offending topic was the "metaphysics of the body" (the school would go on to award Yannaras an honorary doctorate in theology in 2017). A second attempt at a doctorate, this time in France and in philosophy, met with success. It was the years spent studying in Germany and France that led to the discovery of prominent *Western* thinkers who were to have a formative influence on Yannaras' intellectual development: Heidegger, Marx, Wittgenstein, Sartre, and Lacan. Many of Yannaras' monographs engage the ideas of one or more of these thinkers, for example, Heidegger in *Person and Eros* (translated),[xv] Wittgenstein and Lacan in *The Effable and the Ineffable* (translated),[xvi] and Marx in *Rationalism and Social Practice* (untranslated).[xvii] Although they play a lesser role in the present work, Yannaras' most important Eastern Orthodox influences are Maximus the Confessor and the Areopagite writings.

A second attempt at a PhD in theology followed at the Aristotle University of Thessaloniki, this time finding an enthusiastic and positive reception. The work submitted on this occasion would form the basis for the aforementioned *Person and Eros*, with a young Rowan Williams discovering the thesis and producing the first English language engagement with Yannaras' thought in 1972.[xviii]

However, two doctorates—one in philosophy and one in theology—did not facilitate a smooth transition into an academic career in Greece for Yannaras. And when a professorship did eventually come, it was not in theology, but at the Panteion University of Social and Political Sciences in the Department of Political Science and International Studies. What's more, the appointment was bitterly opposed by colleagues and was only finalized after a rather extraordinary saga lasting several years, including student interruptions of committee proceedings, public denunciations from academics at Panteion,

---

xv Christos Yannaras, *Τὸ πρόσωπο καὶ ὁ Ἔρως* 8th ed. (Athens: Ikaros, 2017); Christos Yannaras, *Person and Eros*, trans. Norman Russel (Brookline, MA: Holy Cross Orthodox Press, 2008).
xvi Christos Yannaras, *Τὸ ρητὸ καὶ τὸ ἄρρητο: Τὰ γλωσσικὰ ὅρια ρεαλισμοῦ τῆς μεταφυσικῆς* 2nd ed. (Athens: Ikaros, 2008); Christos Yannaras, *The Effable and the Ineffable: The Linguistic Boundaries of Metaphysical Realism*, trans. Jonathan Cole, ed. and with an intro. Andreas Andreopoulos (Winchester: Winchester University Press, 2021).
xvii Yannaras, *Ὀρθὸς λόγος καὶ κοινωνικὴ πρακτική* [*Rationalism and Social Practice*].
xviii Rowan Williams, "The Theology of Personhood: A Study of the Thought of Christos Yannaras," *Sobornost* 6 (1972): 415–30.

and eleventh-hour attempts to scuttle the appointment at the Ministry of Education. The saga even became front-page news throughout Greece in the early 1980s, with some commentators viewing the episode as a scandalous indictment of corruption in the tertiary sector in Greece. Ironically, Yannaras' background in theology—a fraternity that found him too controversial—contributed to the opposition to his appointment among leftist academics and students at Panteion because it automatically made him a right-wing reactionary in their eyes. The heat eventually passed, however, and Yannaras would go on to have a fruitful twenty-year career at Panteion, where he remains an Emeritus Professor.[xix]

Yannaras is conscious that the meaning of politics is chosen, not given, a fact evident in the synchronic and diachronic variability and contestability of both human political organization and human thought *about* political organization. The meaning, or perhaps better meaning*s*, we humans give to politics is always, in Yannaras' perspective, a reflection of deep, sometimes unconscious, ontological presuppositions. All political organization and political thought are really forms of ontology, although this fact is often obscured in contemporary Western political thought and practice with its pretentions to an objective, efficient, and rational political organization, institutional arrangement, laws, and policies, not to mention its incessant polling, economic modeling, think tank ecosystem, and the so-called science of politics taught and studied in universities.

Yannaras' insight, an ancient one found in the classical Greek tradition of political philosophy, is that our organizational ideas and political concepts come from somewhere, and that somewhere is our deepest perceptions about the reality we collectively inhabit as human beings. It is these deep perceptions, or indeed misperceptions, of reality that determine the telos that we accord our collective (political) life, along with normative proposals for reform and improvement in our political organization. All politics, as far as Yannaras is concerned, whether actual or theoretical, is fundamentally an expression of ontology, or perhaps an expression of ontological longing and desire, if not fear and insecurity. As such, *On the "Meaning" of Politics* is best understood as a meditation on political ontology. Indeed, one of the book's contributions is to direct our attention to the deeply embedded, yet often hidden, and rarely discussed, ontological presuppositions that shape so much of our political discourse and political action today in the West. Yannaras wants us to understand that Western political problems are existential problems, not technical or scientific problems.

The purpose of this meditation is not to offer the one true ideological paradigm that can be imposed on collective human life as though *political* truth consists of a perfect set of institutional forms and relations. On the contrary,

---

xix The saga of Yannaras' professorial appointment at Panteion is recounted in Christos Yannaras, *Τὰ καθ'ἑαυτὸν* [*Memoires*] 4th ed. (Athens: Ikaros, 2005), 158–73.

Yannaras invites us to reconceive politics as a communal process in which, and through which, humans can collectively discover the truth of the cosmos, and then live in a way that is in harmony with that reality. This makes the purpose of politics, in Yannaras' vision, no less than the discovery of truth itself. "Truth" here—*alitheia*—is given the etymological sense of "unhidden," in a contrast to the rationalistic Western conception of truth as objective and accurate information (also the common meaning of *alitheia* in Modern Greek). Truth, in this sense, entails the collective discovery of reality through the convergence of individual experiences of reality intersubjectively communicated and verified via a shared system of signifiers, language.

However, humans are capable of, even predisposed towards, delusion, error, self-deception, and the projection of individual fears and desires, making politics, in actual fact, a perpetual and vital contest between truth and falsehood. Just as politics—the communal life of the *polis*—can reveal the truth, so too can it deceive, particularly if a rationalistic epistemology shapes political thought and organization, underpinned by an individualistic anthropology. This is the great error of the Western political tradition, in Yannaras' estimation, which mistakenly equates truth with linguistic propositions and dehumanizes the personhood of human beings by treating them merely as biological individuals with selfish needs, wants, and interests that must be satisfied and managed amidst competition and rivalry.

Yannaras begins *On the "Meaning" of Politics* by noting an apparent contradiction intrinsic to the "political phenomenon" (Yannaras, in keeping with the conceptual tradition of ancient Greek, always uses the term "political" (*politikos*) as the adjective of *polis*). The contradiction rests in the primordial individualistic nature of the human being, which determines human needs in such a way that appears to ensure inter-human rivalry and conflict, on the one hand, and yet the evident ability of human beings to transcend their individualistic biological natures to share their needs in common, thus forming political communities, on the other.

This contradiction flows out of the dual nature of the human being, as Yannaras sees it—a composite of necessity and freedom, here construed as two distinct modes of existence. Individual human existence is governed by certain necessities that manifest in impulses and urges—passions, in an older conceptuality. Freedom, on the other hand, signifies an existential potentiality open to all individual human beings to exercise their will, to be creative, to construct, and ultimately to express, manifest, and demonstrate truth.

Yannaras identifies three historical models that emerged as means of establishing and maintaining social cohesion amidst the inherent destructive individualistic tendencies of the human species: the first established cohesion by a decree vested with the status of divine law (the dominant historical model), the second established cohesion in consent (the putative social contract), and the third established cohesion by aligning political organization with the truth, which is to say "the commonly verified *mode* in which the given cosmic reality is structured and operates." *On the "Meaning" of Politics* argues that the West is mired in the second model and needs to recapture and restore the third model, which existed as a historical reality (achievement) and continuity from ancient Greek democracy to the ecclesial politics (*polis*-life) of Christian Hellenism.

In this third model, politics is conceived and practiced as a form of collective life that aspires to exist in harmony with the ordered beauty of the cosmos. This telos is predicated on a conception of the world as constituted by *logos*-possessing relations that find their origin in the *logos* that is the first cause of existence (God). *Logos* is an integral concept in all of Yannaras' philosophical and theological writings. It is a difficult concept to grasp that has no English equivalent and encompasses multiple English concepts usually deemed to be semantically distinct, including, *inter alia*, reason, speech, communication, expression, and logic. By the term *logos*, Yannaras points to that quality of reality that gives the universe a profound sense of relational structure, which is to say an order of relations that exist beyond the human being, yet which are knowable to the human, and which also make it possible for the human being, as a *logos*-possessing creature, to participate in that structure. Individual humans can objectively apprehend this structure of relations by virtue of the communicative potential of *logos*, that is, the aforementioned ability to share convergent experiences via a shared language. Yannaras' emphasis on the reality and function of *logos* in the structure of human reality is one element (along with the importance of the *ecclesia*—see below) that adds a vital theological and Eastern Orthodox element to Yannaras' political thought. It is also what brings his meditation on political ontology within the scope of political theology, although that is not a characterization that Yannaras would necessarily accept himself.[xx]

Yannaras identifies two notable historical exceptions (instances of the third model) that managed to avoid the constant and pervasive human temptation to exploit metaphysics as a tool for sacralizing the coercive needs and interests of rulers: the Hebrew and Greek peoples. The Hebrew law given to Moses by Yahweh served not only to provide cohesion and order to Hebrew society, but also expressed and manifested their identity as the chosen people of God. As for the Greeks, they discovered that the best way to meet individual needs was to share them communally via "mutual service." Political authority, in this

---

xx Yannaras was a relatively early critic of political theology, here in its 1970s confessional, not Schmittian, sense, seeing it (correctly at the time) as a Western Christian discourse exhibiting Western theological and social concerns and, in Yannaras' view, Western theological pathologies, such as a narrow focus on the "social utility" of the gospel rather than the transcendent and existential horizon of the relationship between the church and politics. See Christos Yannaras, "A Note on Political Theology," trans. Peter Tsichlis, *St Vladimir's Theological Quarterly* 27, no. 1 (1983): 53–6.

context, was conceived as a *leitourgima*, which is to say, a "public service." Yannaras contends that the original (liturgical) understanding of authority as a service for, and on behalf of, the people degenerated into an office of prestige, all-too-often exercised by an individual for, or on behalf of, that individual's own interests, which is to say in tyrannical modes.

Yannaras posits an epistemological drive behind the emergence of the Greek model of politics as a "communion of truth." It was the Greek understanding of the need to distinguish between truth and falsehood that led to the notion of a communitarian epistemology served by the collective existence of the *polis* (politics). The Greeks came to understand that knowledge possessed by an individual and not shared with the community was unreliable, thus giving birth to the insight that politics (*polis*-life) constituted a primary vehicle for the discovery of truth. According to Yannaras, the great truth discovered by Greek *political* life was that the mode of existence is unchanging, incorruptible, and eternal. While individual existents come and go, live and die, the mode in which they exist endures. It is *logos* that provides this continuity of existence, which Yannaras describes, quoting Heraclitus, as the "mode by which the universe is governed."

On the basis of this Greek communitarian epistemology, one can begin to see that the *polis*, as a large and concentrated collective life of many individuals sharing their individual needs, becomes the principal vehicle by which humans can discover the truth—uncovering that which otherwise would remain hidden, on Yannaras' etymological understanding of the Greek word for truth, *a-litheia* (unhidden). In Yannaras' theo-philosophical vision, the truth discovered by the *actual* Greek experience of collective life in the *polis* was that truth is not a thing, but rather a way, which is to say a mode of existence that is "timeless, incorruptible, immutable, and immortal."

However, the Greeks, in their pre-Christian incarnation, had one serious blind spot: they were ignorant of the personal, relational, loving Trinitarian God who exists in freedom—a first cause that "exists because he *wills* to exist, and he wills to exist because he *loves*." As a consequence, the telos of *political* life in pre-Christian Greece amounted to the pursuit of truth construed as living in accord with the impersonal rational harmony of a given universe that existed out of necessity. With the Greek embrace of Christianity, however, with its *ecclesial* event testifying to a Trinitarian God who causes existence out of a loving freedom, not necessity, the telos of *political* coexistence became life lived in communion with the Trinitarian mode of existence, what Yannaras calls the "Trinitarian archetype of politics."

Yannaras stresses that this Greek (both pagan and Christian) conception of politics as a communion of shared need, the collective struggle to discover truth, and the aspiration to live in harmony with the mode by which the universe is governed, existed as a continuous historical reality from the time of the ancient Greek *polis* to the self-governing communities of Byzantium, with *ecclesia* marking a key axis of continuity—the *ecclesia* (assembly) of the people (*demos*) in Athenian democracy becoming the *ecclesia* (gathering) of the faithful (*piston*) in the Christian church.[xxi] The unique historical achievement of Greek political life came to an end, in the Greek context, with the fall of Constantinople in 1453 and the birth four centuries later of the modern Greek state which embraced Western conceptions of politics and sought to mimic Western modes of political organization.

However, this Greek-Christian mode of politics came to an end in Western Christianity much earlier, and in ways that have shaped the contemporary culture of much of the world. The collapse of the Western Roman empire and the embrace of Christianity by invading and settling Germanic tribes perverted the *ecclesial* event into a religion. The "ecclesial event" in this context describes the new mode of existence inaugurated by the union of the created and uncreated in the incarnation of the historical person Jesus Christ, subsequently embodied in the communion of need that is the *ecclesia*. Religion, in Yannaras' account, privileges the individual over the collective, thus representing a degeneration of the communion-centered nature implicit in the concept of *ecclesia*. The Christian religion, with this seminal turn in the historical and cultural development of Europe, began to emphasize beliefs, obedience, and individual salvation. The legacy of Christianity as a religion is the (mis)understanding of democracy in deontological or ideological terms—a question of the best form of political organization possible for meeting material ends, which is to say a matter of utility and efficacy. This forms a stark contrast, and tension, with the original Greek understanding of democracy, along with its Christian *ecclesial* version, as a relational communion that serves to uncover the true reality of (shared) existence.

Yannaras laments the fact that the rampant individualism that is a product of Western religion has distorted the meaning of democracy for contemporary citizens. Democracy is now understood primarily through the lens of individual rights, obscuring, if not making it impossible, for many citizens to apprehend the ontological and epistemological implications, and potential of politics—our collective life together. The same fate has befallen the Christian *ecclesia*, which now functions as a religion, including in the Orthodox East, promising individual salvation and functioning much like any other political ideology—dogmatic, militant, and inflexible. The very word at the heart of "politics," *polis*, has also degenerated from a communion of need aspiring to the collective discovery of truth to a comparative quantitative entity, that is, a collection of individuals living in one concentrated geographic location that is bigger than either a town or village (*polis* means "city" in Modern Greek in the same sense as the English term). Today, politics has thoroughly lost its ontological horizon, devolving into little more than a mechanism for

---

xxi This plays on the fact that the Greek word for church, *ecclesia* (ἐκκλησία), was the same word used for assembly in Athenian democracy.

sharing power, passing laws, and solving coordination and distribution challenges. Worse still, the individualism unleashed by religion leads, according to Yannaras, to forms of political totalitarianism, as witnessed to destructive effect in twentieth century Europe. Such totalitarianisms are propped up and maintained through the imposition of unitary ideologies that assume the function of religion, namely, the enforcement and policing of uniform dogmas intolerant of dissent.

Some readers may feel inclined to protest that Yannaras' meditation on politics is too cursory, schematic, and broad-brush to constitute an acceptable historical and philosophical account of the development and nature of Western civilization (and religion). But *On the "Meaning" of Politics* is not offered as a systematic study of Western civilization, nor is it a detailed manifesto for political reform. It is a provocation designed to evoke readers living in Western political cultures (initially Yannaras' Greek compatriots, now a wider English-speaking audience) to look deeper for the sources of their political problems. It is an invitation to recognize and re-examine the ontological and epistemological presuppositions which shape Western political institutions, ideas, and practices in the hope that citizens of Western liberal democracies might reconceive their politics as a vital struggle to collectively discover and realize the truth of existence. Those prepared to read the provocation in the spirit of imagination identified by Williams in his foreword will find *On the "Meaning" of Politics* not only stimulating, but rewarding.

1 Reverence and justice

By studying the historical development of the political phenomenon, which is to say the historical forms of organized human coexistence, we can form logical, if hypothetical, conclusions about its origins—the original needs and motivations that led to the genesis of political society. Confident in our ability to reason, albeit without absolute certainty, we can work our way back from history to pre-history.

The myth preserved by Protagoras, reiterated by Plato, attributes the origin and beginning of the political event to a transcendent factor, to a *sacred* beginning:

> Men dwelt separately in the beginning, and *poleis* there were none; so that they were being destroyed by the wild beasts, since these were in all ways stronger than they; and although their skill in handiwork was a sufficient aid in respect of food, in their warfare with the beasts it was defective; for as yet they had no political art [the presuppositions for coexistence], which includes the art of war. So they sought to band themselves together and secure their lives by founding *poleis*. Now as often as they were banded together, they did wrong to one another through the lack of political art, and thus they began to be scattered again and to perish. So Zeus, fearing that our race was in danger of utter destruction, sent Hermes to bring reverence [self-respect, restraint, aversion to scandal, dignity] and justice [the mode of rational order and propriety, as well as their imposition] among men, to the end that there should be regulation of *poleis* and friendly ties to draw them together.[i]

This myth or echo, perhaps even product, of common experience takes the centrality of the human individual to be primordially given—it assumes this to be the *mode* in which humans exist. Collective life (organized coexistence) constitutes an epiphenomenon, something accomplished, not primordially given—it is not a product of human *nature*, but a gift from the gods, that is, a freedom achieved in spite of human *nature*.

---

i Plato, *Protagoras*, trans. and rev. W.R.M. Lamb (London: William Heinemann, 1937), 322 b1–c3. Adapted. Square brackets Yannaras'.

DOI: 10.4324/9781003410867-2

Organized coexistence (life constituted in a *polis*, i.e., *political* life), as told by the myth, is bestowed upon humans by the gods as a prerequisite for their continued existence. Coexistence, although not a product of human *nature*, serves as a necessary condition for its preservation. It is therefore a precondition of the existence of that nature. Individualistic by *nature*, the human being survives as a *natural* species only because the individuals that belong to that *natural species* transcend their *natural* individualism and share their needs in common. They share the burden of defense against external enemies, and they manage in common their vital needs through the development of specialized knowledge and activities.

Human existence (the common *mode* in which humans exist, their *nature—essence*) thus appears to embody a contradiction, a kind of bipolarity or existential schizophrenia: humans are primevally governed by individual needs (instincts, urges, and appetites) that are independent of any other existential operation; yet at the same time, the *mode* in which humans exist is largely determined by given non-instinctive existential operations, such as reason, will, imagination, intuition, and symbolic meaning. "Non-instinctive" is to say operations that do not function as impersonal (undifferentiated) necessities, but which realize and manifest the *otherness* (existential uniqueness and distinctness) characteristic of every individual existence, alongside undifferentiated instincts.

2 Necessity and freedom

Human existence can also be described as having a *dual nature*. The reality of existence is comprised of two composite natures, which is to say two *modes* of existence: *necessity* and *freedom*. Individualistic urges, as irrepressible necessities, come into conflict with the free and unpredetermined operations of actualized human otherness—reason, will, imagination, and symbolic expression. An individual existence is subject to (*suffers*) the necessities that govern it. The name we give to the laws that determine human nature is passions. The antithesis of passions, in terms of both experience and conceptuality, is freedom. Freedom could be defined and signified as the ability to distinguish and differentiate existential *potential* from existential *necessity*.

Experientially, freedom is to be found in the realm of volition (will); it determines and delimits the choices open to will. It is more than this, however. Creative potential (making, building) is also a form of freedom from natural necessity, although it is susceptible to the natural impulse towards narcissism. Freedom can, however, transcend narcissism and foster a love for beauty (via art). In turn, the language of beauty can serve to express, manifest, and demonstrate *truth*. Freedom is also capable of establishing existential self-transcendence and loving self-offering, across a broad spectrum ranging from sympathy to self-sacrifice.

The fact that the natural necessities which govern human existence are centered on the individual undermines collective life and coexistence. Freedom from instinctive drives and passions, and their restraint by reason and will, are prerequisites for an organized common life. Cognizance of these two foundational insights leads one to see the necessity of establishing freedom via decree, applied coercively and universally. Such a set of circumstances can come into existence in one of three ways or via three paths: 1) a decree vested in a *transcendent* authority, for example, the will of God (the supreme cause and beginning of what exists), and thus given the status of divine *law*; 2) a decree enacted by common agreement or contract in the form of a *law* or as the condition for participation in the collective, with penalties for noncompliance; or 3) the decree could be identified with the *truth*, which is to

DOI: 10.4324/9781003410867-3

say with the commonly verified *mode* in which the given cosmic reality is structured and operates, a *mode* that is unchanging, incorruptible, and eternal. These three *modes* of, or *paths* towards, constraining individualism as a means of making the social (political) event feasible have given shape to three historical forms of organized human coexistence. The first form is where authority and metaphysics, state and religion, and the impact of the transcendent on organized collective life are organically interwoven and co-emergent. The second form is where political cohabitation is secularized, which is to say, where political cohabitation is separated from any form of metaphysical authority, model, or deontology, and which is founded exclusively on the instrumental logic of utilitarianism, and in due course on the functionality of common human reason. The third form is the Greek *polis*, political (*polis*) life, democracy (rule by the people), where the goal of coexistence, cohabitation, and organized collective life is attainment of the *true mode of existence* via the communal sharing of need. Collective life, in the Greek *polis*, constituted a *mode* of communally sharing needs and relationships *according to logos*[i] (harmony, ornamental order[ii]), in other words, according to the shape of the universe's eternal and unchanging *order*.

These three forms of organized human coexistence are explored further in the chapters that follow.

---

i Translator's note: *logos*, the most common Modern Greek meaning of which is "reason," is a notoriously polysemic term in both Modern Greek and Ancient Greek. Yannaras uses *logos* in a distinctive sense that is untranslatable in English: that which reveals what someone or something is and allows access to knowledge of it as a consequence of that revelation. *Logos* therefore captures a number of distinct English concepts that should be read together in the context of the present work, including logic, reason, principle, cause, speech, communication, and gesture.

ii Translator's note: *kosmiotita*, an untranslatable term that connotes both order and beauty, and which is used by Yannaras to describe the way in which the totality of existents exist, that is, in a mode that is ordered, harmonious, and beautiful. It is translated as "ornamentality" in cases where it appears in close proximity to the term *taxi*, which also means "order," albeit without the connotations of beauty.

3 Forms of organized coexistence

Form 1: *organized human cohabitation established by, and cohering in, a religio-metaphysical axis.*
The origins of the close connection between *authority* and *religion* in collective human life look destined to remain lost in the depths of pre-history: they appear to be inherently interwoven, not brought together.

A fundamental feature of human perception is the relationship between *cause* and *effect* that is obvious to everyone. Perception functions in the mind in a deterministic movement from the specific to the general, from the general to the universal, and from effect to cause. The saying "for every house is built by someone, but the builder of all things is God" (Heb. 3:4) vividly encapsulates the logic of this self-evident reduction of every existent to its cause, and of all that exists to an initial first cause of existence.

The sequential chain of cause and effect makes the existence of a *first cause* of everything logically clear (necessary): a creative origin (commencement, beginning) of what is given in reality. However, it is just as logically clear (obvious) that a *cause* is connected to some *purpose* or goal. The relationship between *cause* and *purpose* also belongs to the given *logos-mode* in which human perception functions: a *purposeless* (or *irrational*) existence can be conceived intellectually, but only as the product of imagination. It lacks the unmediated clarity of what is self-evident to all, or empirically obvious.

By the same token, the fact that the first cause is self-evidently connected to some purposive *end* not only endows the products of its creation with evidence of an originating *logikotita*,[i] but also a *regulatory* quality. A fundamental feature of human perception is that it functions in such a way that not only connects (via immediate, self-evident lucidity) the concept of a *first cause* with the *creation* and genesis of existents (their ex nihilo emergence into existence), but also with the *preservation*, providence, and wise foresight

---

i Translator's note: *logikotita* in Modern Greek means "rationality." However, in this context it is an untranslatable word by virtue of its connection to Yannaras' distinctive sense of *logos*. Its literal sense in English might be something approximate to *logos*-ness.

DOI: 10.4324/9781003410867-4

of the preconditions by which existents endure. That existents are *created* and *preserved* is empirically and universally self-evident and can also be deduced logically—to question otherwise would cast doubt on our commonly verified experience of existents as they are given.

Every aspect of *existent* (presence) and *existential* (mode) reality is embedded in a nexus of *originating* causes, and also *preserved* (regulatory preconditions) through *logos*. By *logos*-possessing[ii] "nexus," we mean to say a nexus of *relations*—the existent is known and determined (distinguished) by virtue of its incorporation in this nexus. The *relations* between existents are logical and analogical (according to *logos* and through *logos*). In this way existents are also *phenomena*, which is to say apparent and manifest (see Heraclitus: "the thing that appears to all in common, that is what is believable").[iii]

The reality of the universe's phenomenal appearance, that is, the *logos*-relations of existents, points to an original *logos*—the precondition (cause) and purpose (regulation) of the universe's *logos*-relations. By identifying the *logos*-mode in which existents *exist* with the *logos*-mode in which humans *apprehend* reality (i.e., identifying apprehension with the way in which phenomena appear, and the appearance of phenomena with *logos*-relations), we can attribute some rational properties to the *logos* which brings into being and regulates the very existence that is the reality of the universe. This is to say that we can attempt to reach a rational (shared) comprehension of the first cause of existence itself.

If we assume that existence is a positive predicate, in contrast to its privative antithesis "non-existence," then our endeavor to arrive at a fulsome understanding of the first cause of existence can really only begin from one place: the infinite regress of positive properties that common human logic recognizes in what is caused by the first cause. Thus, we trace backwards (regress) from *caused* existence to *uncaused* existence *per se*, and from there to the incorruptibility, omniscience, omnipotence, and so forth, of the first cause.

---

ii Translator's note: *logiko*, the adjectival form of *logos*. *Logos*-possessing has been chosen throughout as the best option among a suite of imperfect solutions in order to retain the adjectival sense of *logos*.
iii Heraclitus, *Die Fragmente der Vorsokratiker I*, eds. Hermann Diels and Walther Kranz (Berlin: Weidmannsche Verlagsbuchhandlung, 1952), 148, 22.

4 Cohesion through coercion

Although the paradigmatic observations made in the previous chapter are only indicative, they do provide a sufficient basis upon which to apprehend the archetypal image of what it is for human cohabitation to be organized according to *logos*. The image, by virtue of being archetypal, is unavoidably drawn from our observation, contemplation, and experience of the ornamental order of existents in their totality and as they are given: coexistence is stable and has continuity when it constitutes a cosmos, the ornamentality of *logos*-possessing harmony and order. Harmony and order point to a first cause which, by its effect, can be characterized as cosmos-making, and hence as *regulating*. As such, the archetypal model of human collective life, given its analogical relation to the natural universe, is undoubtedly *monarchic*. A single cause[i] coheres and regulates the whole. Coherence, like the *rationality* of ornamental order, possesses a *sacred* character, which is to say that it is generative of life. The monarch (king or sovereign) officiates over the rites of life, as a kind of priestly work, bringing about cohesion and ornamental order. For life—a form of sacredness par excellence—only becomes feasible within a cohesive communion[ii] of need and relational harmony.

All forms of authority in human collective existence arise from the need to safeguard a life of communion and harmony. That is why the exercise of power can be characterized as a *leitourgima*—a service for the common good. *Leitourgima* is a compound of "people" (*laos*) and "work" (*ergon*), namely a work of the people, a work for the benefit of the people and in the service of all, a work of the demos, a public work, a work in the public interest.

---

i Translator's note: *Mia archi*, literally "one cause." *Archi* also means origin, principle, and rule, and can be read with these connotations in this context. In the first instance, *mia archi* relates back to *monarchiki* in the previous sentence, which literally means "lone-rule." I have translated *archi* in this context as "cause" in order to connect the concept with first cause earlier, which is the conventional English translation of *Proti Archi*.

ii Translator's note: *koinonia*, translated throughout as communion and connected to the verb *koinono*, translated variously as "share," "share in common," and "communally share."

DOI: 10.4324/9781003410867-5

However, it is a fact of common human experience that a social *leitourgima* (in the sense of servicing common needs) can degenerate (with surprising ease) into a rigid individual-centered *office*. This degeneration also arises from need, albeit not from the need to safeguard a life of communion and harmony, but from the unconscious innate needs of the natural individual (led by instinctive drives rather than reason): drives of the ego.

Freud came to use the term "life-drives" (*Lebenstriebe*) to describe these manifestations of the human propensity or tendency to form and retain unities (i.e., unifying totalities, organized forms, universal receptions). These unifying drives can also be signified by the term *eros*, here covering not only sexual drives, but also those of self-preservation. Freud used the term "death-drives" (*Todestriebe*) to describe manifestations of the human propensity or tendency (found in every living organism) "to return to an inorganic state." In the first place, death-drives are introspective, inclined towards individual autonomy, and thus to non-communion. They possess a self-destructive character (for the living existent), which imprisons them in the atomicity of a narcissistic false sense of security, thus isolating them from the connectivity of vital relations that preserve the existence of the entire biological ecosystem. In the second place, death-drives become outwardly focused on the form of aggression, destructiveness, domination, and the desire for power.

5 *Leitourgima's* degeneration into office

The degeneration of *leitourgima* (a service for the common good) into *office* has generated a proliferation of institutionalized forms of authority. These degenerate forms of authority can be categorized according to designations that correspond more or less with the ethos of the officer holder and less so, if at all, with fixed types of polity. What I have in mind is *monarchy* (*kingship*, *despotism*, or *satrapy*), *hegemony*, *tyranny*, and *absolutism*.

Of interest to our inquiry is the fact that, irrespective of the moral quality or specific shape taken by institutions of authority, their religious foundation appears to have been initially self-evident (and for many centuries thereafter). Securing good order, a legal regime of justice, collective cohesion, and solidarity were all dependent on the acceptance of some divine command, or the translation of a divine will into regulating principles for cohabitation or the transcendent prestige of established legislation. The norm in human history (possibly the rule) has been for metaphysics to lend instrumental validity to the ordinances which regulate common life, instead of illuminating the *meaning* (cause and aim) of existence and existents.

As a general rule, metaphysics (perspective, reflection, inquiry) has been subordinated to the priority of utility and not to the thirst for truth, notwithstanding notable exceptions. One such notable exception is the people of Israel, and more specifically the *Mosaic Law*: commands and regulations which, according to Hebrew tradition, Moses received from God and conveyed to the people of Israel as a guide for its behavior and life. The commands of the Mosaic Law determined what was necessary (propriety and duty), albeit not as an instrumental end in itself or merely to facilitate well-ordered cohabitation. Obeying the law's commands was a practical means by which the Hebrew people could consciously understand, declare, and manifest their membership as the people of Israel, a people chosen by God—chosen so that God's relationship with the whole of humanity might be disclosed and made manifest. Obeying the Mosaic Law did not provide Hebrews individual reward; it simply made it tangibly clear that they belonged—an active and steadfast faith in their election as God's people. By virtue of the law, this participation was genuinely free, not biologically (genetically) given.

DOI: 10.4324/9781003410867-6

22 Leitourgima's *degeneration into office*

A second notable exception is the Greek people, a people which came to the realization before any other that *need* is always best met "mutually,"[i] always via mutual service: "sharing in common need." In this way, *need* becomes "man's teacher."[ii] It guides (teaches) humans in the art of survival—"the discoveries of a necessary kind are probably taught by need itself."[iii] It teaches what is required for the satisfaction of human need—collective *cohesion* is essential to organized coexistence. Need coheres (binds together) all who partake in collective life: "For if humans had absolutely no need at all, or if their needs were not the same, then either there would be no exchange, or no exchange would be the same."[iv]

However, *need*—the totality of essentials that governs (defines and binds) human existence—does not infer irrational (non-*logos*) or mechanistic necessity, nor "fate." Coexistence and need are both "in-*logos*"[v] (according to *logos*, ana*logical*), such that when needs are shared in common, they establish coexistence. "In-*logos*" here means intentional, purposeful, serving its rational end, not as a secondary goal, but as the primary goal of existence. "In-*logos*" also means realized *according to logos*, that is, via the mode of *relations*—*logos*-possessing relations of mutual fulfillment, harmony, order, and ornamentality. Hence, the need that provides the cohesion for human coexistence is *logos*-possessing in the same way as the need that coheres and elevates the reality of the universe into a *cosmos* (ornament) of harmony, good order, and beauty.

The need that provides the cohesion for human coexistence participates in the comprehensive *logos*-relations that bind together, connect, or tune the ordered (cosmic) universe—the *logos*-possessing "mode of universal governance"[vi] that is both necessary for, and a condition of, the universe's ornamental order. The Greek experience of observing and contemplating the cosmic whole certifies that the reality of the universe exists and functions according to *logos*: the *logos-mode* in which existents exist (down to the immortal gods) is, logically and inexplicably, given and predetermined. Every existent exists (and coexists) in a predetermined manner obedient to the truth of the immortal, incorruptible, and immutable (and inexplicably given) *logos-mode*.

The Greek exception constitutes the third form (or type) of human coexistence. It can be apprehended more clearly by bringing into view its conceptual (and actual) antithesis, the second form, which consequentially refused to find refuge in the authority of either the omnipotence and sacredness of the metaphysical factor or the validity of *authentic truth*.

---

i Plato, *Republic Books 1–5*, trans. and ed. Chris Emlyn-Jones and William Preddy (Cambridge: Harvard University Press, 2013), II, 372a.
ii Democritus, *Die Fragmente der Vorsokratiker II*, eds. Hermann Diels and Walther Kranz (Berlin: Weidmannsche Verlagsbuchhandlung, 1952), 136, 12–13.
iii Aristotle, *Politics*, trans. H. Rackham (Cambridge: Harvard University Press, 1944), VII 1329b 27.
iv Aristotle, *The Nichomachean Ethics*, trans. and rev. H Rackham (Cambridge: Harvard University Press, 1934), V.11. Translator's note: the English translation is of Yannaras' Modern Greek translation of Aristotle.
v Translator's note: *ellogi*, a literal translation.
vi Heraclitus, *Die Fragmente der Vorsokratiker I*, 148, 29.

6 *Ratio* dethrones authority

The second type or form of organized human coexistence emerged out of the rejection of all metaphysical authority, models, and metaphysically enshrined deontology. In this form, organized human coexistence is founded constitutionally in the instrumental logic of utilitarianism, the functionality of common logic, and the efficacy of convention.

Historically speaking, this type did not emerge in the primordial phase of human development. It was the predictable product of collective resistance to the arbitrary exercise of authority and the demands of a religiously defined hegemony. Ernst Wolfgang Böckenförde (b. 1930), in his invaluable study, *The Emergence of the State as a Process of Secularization*,[i] broadly (though correctly) identified the medieval societies of the West as the source of rupture that saw the emergence of a mature need for the consistent separation of political authority from religious authority.

Böckenförde's study succumbs to the temptation of attributing the contingent historical circumstances manifest in the medieval West to universal necessities and generic anthropological constants. This attribution is clearly arbitrary, albeit in such a way that is not obvious, for out of these specific circumstances there emerged a radically new and unprecedented civilizational paradigm with an extremely effective global dynamism. These contingent circumstances were a consequence of the extraordinary migration of barbarian tribes and hordes (then at a primitive level of collective development and individual cultivation) to the Western provinces of the Roman Empire (from the fourth to the sixth centuries AD). These circumstances were deemed, in retrospect, to have been the consequence of permanent historical necessities and generic anthropological constants. The barbarian paradigm prevailed against the Greek and Greco-Roman paradigms, manifestly shaping the terms in which we understand and evaluate the relationship between political authority and metaphysics.

---

i Ernst Wolfgang Böckenförde, *Die Entstehung des Staates als Vorgang der Säkularisation*, (Stuttgart: Kohlhammer Verlag, 1967).

DOI: 10.4324/9781003410867-7

24 Ratio *dethrones authority*

Thus, in medieval (post-Roman) Europe, the relationship between religion and political authority became a Procrustean interpretive crutch for the purposes of understanding the relationship between religion and authority, diachronically and universally. In the perspective of what is now a global Western paradigm (in terms of mindset, criteria, and established habits), what happened in the barbarian post-Roman Europe of the Middle Ages, with respect to the relationship between politics and religion, is deemed (by analogy) to have occurred also in ancient Greece, ancient China, and the thousand-year empire of the New Rome, Constantinople, that is, always and everywhere.

A characteristic example of this arbitrary interpretation is the need shown by contemporary scholars (including professional historians) to find in modern *representative* democracy a means for understanding (and evaluating) ancient Athenian democracy. This is done by looking for something analogous to the protection of "individual rights," the rationalistic balancing of individual interests, and a common "principle" of universal franchise—instrumental elements of a utilitarianism centered on the individual that did not exist in the mindset of ancient Greeks and was not counted among their needs.[ii]

[ii] Indicative examples of this tragic arbitrariness in contemporary Greek scholarship are the studies of Michail Sakellariou, *Ancient Athenian Democracy* (Heraklion: Crete University Press, 1999) and Cornelius Kastoriadis, *Ancient Greek Democracy and Its Significance for Us Today* (Athens: Ypsilon, 1999).

7 The desire for "salvation" dethrones *ratio*

Böckenförde's study, notwithstanding its misguided interpretive approach, illuminates (albeit clearly unintentionally) some crucial aspects of the relationship between authority and metaphysics in the medieval West. He writes that "the empire [in reference to the imperial ambitions of Charlemagne and his successors] did not live off the imperial inheritance of Rome."[i] The Roman inheritance continued organically only in the New Rome, Constantinople—a second international "order of things" (*ordo rerum*) existing in parallel to the universal *pax romana* was universally inconceivable. For precisely this reason, the newly established barbarian West treated the empire of *Nova Roma* (Constantinople) as a much despised rival: it stood in the way of its own ambitions for international dominance.

The one cohesive element of the Greco-Roman "world"[ii] (*pax romana*) that could be transmuted without leading to the dissolution of the empire's cohesion was its *religio imperii*. The Greco-Roman imperium passed from emperor worship (*cultus imperatorius*) to religious toleration (the edict of Milan, 313 AD), and from there to Christianity (Theodosius I, 380) without losing the presuppositions of the Roman international *ordo rerum*.

The barbarian post-Roman West lacked the presuppositions necessary to function under the terms of a "universal" (in Greek, "catholic") empire. Perhaps it thought it was imitating the function of the *religio imperii* when the leaders of the invading barbarian tribes were baptized as Christians (followed by the mass baptism of their people in rivers). Yet, in reality they merely continued what they had known, which was to attribute sacredness and transcendent authority to the legal rulings and decisions of their leader, no doubt because of the instrumental and utilitarian efficacy of authority.

---

i Böckenförde, *Die Entstehung des Staates als Vorgang der Säkularisation*, (the quotation is from a Greek translation by Petro Giatzakis in *Neo Planodion* 3 (2015): 71).
ii Translator's note: *oikoumene*.

DOI: 10.4324/9781003410867-8

8 *Ecclesia* and religion
Incompatible modes of existence

The Christianized barbarian tribes were completely unaware of the antithetical difference between *Ecclesia*[i] and *religion*, between life and existence as an ecclesial event of *communion* and individualistic religiosity. They sacralized the exercise of authority and demanded a coercive power for the *Ecclesia* because for them, Christianity, as Böckenförde crucially understood,

> had as its mission the realization of the *regnum Dei*, the kingdom of God on earth, i.e., constraining the assault of evil in the current age . . . Christianity became a public religion, determining the order of daily life. It also assimilated many superstitious and naturalistic elements from the religiosity of the Germanic tribes.

Böckenförde added that

> faith (the totality of individual convictions) assumed the form of a religio-political and juridical relationship: this relationship entailed subordination to a feudal master and obedience to an all-powerful God-king, Christ . . . The ruler was a Christian, and therefore also subject to the Christian commandments. The cleric had responsibility for ensuring the ruler's compliance with the commandments. The popes and cannon lawyers of the Roman curia lent the force of authority to this logic (the accountability of rulers to clerics) . . .

---

i Translator's note: *Ecclesia* (*ekklisia*) means "church" in Modern Greek. However, it becomes clear in Chapters 13 and 14 that *ecclesia* here has a different sense from what is typically understood by the word "church" in English. Indeed it forms a contrast. Yannaras emphasizes the etymological meaning of *ekklisia* as "calling out" and connects it with the *ekklisia* ("assembly") of Athenian democracy. For these reasons I have chosen to render *ekklisia* as "*ecclesia*" throughout, retaining Yannaras' capitalization, and reserving instances of "church" for occasions that clearly relate to the religionized *ecclesia*, a perversion of the true meaning of the *ecclesia* in Yannaras' account.

DOI: 10.4324/9781003410867-9

Ecclesia *and religion* 27

The primacy of spiritual power (popes and clerics) presupposed a commitment to making judgments and determinations on all matters, under the constant prism of *ratione saluti* or *ratione peccati* (the logic of salvation or the logic of sin) . . . *Ratio peccati* is the sole absolute principle to which *ratio ordinis politici* (the logic of good political order) is subordinate . . .

. . . The mission (responsibility and task) of worldly power was to stamp out heresy via its institutions, and to then punish heretics publicly . . . [because] the Christian religion formed the indisputable bedrock or common ground that guaranteed the unity of ruler and subject.[ii]

This kind of suffocating and controlling exercise of temporal authority by religious officials generated a rupture, which, once it had occurred, was literally uncontainable. Political authority sought an uncompromising autonomy and independence by citing two obvious facts: 1) the incessant disputes and fanatical, stubborn, and bloody conflicts caused by dogmatic differences of belief, which manifested in a policy of the persecution and horrific torture of dissent, as well as unrestrained amnesty for the crimes committed by servants of the transcendent; and 2) the rationalism of utilitarianism was conducive to secularization (the liberation of temporal power from priestly control)—the efficacy of utilitarianism formed the backbone of the irreligious administration of the people's collective needs and rights.

In due course, we will revisit this analysis of the characteristics of the second type or form of organized human coexistence, which emerged out of the secularization of politics. Before doing so, however, it is imperative to complete our typology of collective forms by adding the third historical type in order to ensure that our interpretive lens is sufficiently clear. That third type is the form of organized collective life that emerges when the need to realize human coexistence in the mode of *truth*, the mode of existence *according to truth*, becomes a shared priority: a reality that does not perish, does not alter, and does not die. Such a mode can only be the "mode of universal governance" (Heraclitus), the *means*[iii] of the universe's harmony and beauty, coexistence *according to the logos* and *order* of the eternal and immutable reality of the universe.

---

ii Böckenförde, *Die Entstehung des Staates als Vorgang der Säkularisation*, 71–2, 76.
iii Translator's note: *to pos*, literally, "the how."

9 When truth becomes the priority

We encounter the first historical appearance of the third type or form of organized collective life in the Greek *polis*—*political* life and *political virtue*.[i] We previously raised the Greek proposal as an exception (along with the Hebrew Mosaic Law) to the utilitarian model—a metaphysical construal of politics in which metaphysics did not function as an authority ensuring "accuracy,"[ii] but rather entailed a goal desired and pursued for its own sake. That goal was to see the "communion of need" (the needs of subsistence) function as a "communion of truth." We now turn to a more extensive analysis of this Greek proposal, the idiosyncratic (more likely unique) Greek contribution to the organization and function of collective human life.

The Greek model was not religious. It did not seek to valorize the origins and terms of its collective coexistence by lending metaphysical prestige to those who held power and to their rulings (the legal and normative principles of coexistence). The Greek proposal arose from the need of each and every Greek to distinguish and separate reliable from unreliable opinion, testimony, and information, the correct from the mistaken, truth from falsehood. The Greeks sought to discover the "criterion of truth" (Heraclitus). Moreover, as we have already noted, the Greeks certified that this *criterion* is not a *thing*—some existent that is timeless, incorruptible, immutable, and immortal, but a *way*: a *mode* that is timeless, incorruptible, immutable, and immortal—"the mode of universal governance."

This cosmic mode is given, "no god or man made [it], but it always was, is, and will be an everlasting fire, being kindled in measures and being put out in measures."[iii] Being everlasting (immortal), it is the only experientially and universally accessible reality which *is true*. That is why it constitutes the

---

i Translator's note: *Political* here should be read as the adjective of *polis*.
ii Translator's note: *Orthotita*. This is a key concept, which could also be rendered as "correctness" or "rectitude."
iii Heraclitus, *Die Fragmente der Vorsokratiker*, 157–8, 11 & 3. English translation taken from Heraclitus, *Fragments: A Text and Translation with a Commentary by T.M. Robinson* (Toronto: University of Toronto Press, 1987).

DOI: 10.4324/9781003410867-10

criterion of truth. Individual existents are mutable, corruptible, and mortal. However, their *mode* of existence and coexistence is immutable, incorruptible, and immortal. This is existence *according to truth*. The Greeks did not pursue the *criterion of truth* for utilitarian purposes. Rather, it came out of a clear "desire for immortality," a desire and longing for knowledge and experiential participation in the *mode* of the true, in the *event* of truth. In the context of today's global civilizational paradigm (universally and comprehensively dominant), the word *truth* is understood in terms of instrumental and utilitarian accuracy: individual trust in demonstrably (commonly accepted) infallible semantic, significatory, and interpretive codes of the existent and real. Truth as accuracy is open to individual possession (by everyone). It becomes the property of the individual, armor for protecting the ego, a weapon for waging war against denial, adulteration, or doubt of the ego's self-assurance. Truth as accuracy produces individual *beliefs* (individually chosen and determined). The only way to homogenize and harmonize, or at least converge, individual choices and beliefs is to subject the conduits of belief to a single *authority*, or a single *contract*. An authority that enforces from above (axiomatically and dogmatically) correct judgments. In a contract, the contracting parties voluntarily agree to accept the accuracy of specific judgments.

The Greeks represent literally the polar opposite of this example. The word *truth* [*a-litheia*], according to its etymological root (the privative *a-* and *lithi*, "hidden"), meant unhidden, which is to say apparent, revealed, *coming into the light*. The word points to a vital experiential event, an experience of participation in a surrounding reality—not merely an intellectual conception (the Western medieval definition of *truth* as "a correspondence between thought and mind"—*veritas est adaequatio rei et intellectus*—is a repudiation of the Greek tradition and its experiential character).

The Greeks also signified *phenomenon*[iv] (disclosure—manifestation) with the word *logos*: anything that appears *communicates* by its appearance (its form of otherness) *what* it is (e.g., a tree, a bird, or a flower). The word *logos* always signified the disclosure of a *referential* event constitutive of a relation. Anything that appears refers,[v] in other words, comes towards the recipient to whom it is disclosed. That disclosure in turn creates knowledge, knowledge constitutive of an epistemic relationship with the recipient of the phenomenon.

Thus, knowledge of existents and events (of being and becoming) constitutes truth (unhidden) because it arises from the experience of relationships.

---

iv Translator's note: "phenomenon" (*fainomeno*) is the past participle of the Greek verb *faino*, "to appear."

v Translator's note: *ana-feretai*, which means "refer" in Modern Greek, but Yannaras here places a hyphen between its constituent parts to highlight its etymological sense of "brought up" (i.e., raised up).

Knowledge is not formed by intellectual conception alone (the mind's apprehension[vi]). It takes the vital experiential immediacy of relationship to know the existent and event before us. It is no accident that many of the words used in the Greek language to denote the function of knowledge are drawn from the lexical semantics of sight. Greeks spoke of *contemplation, observation, phenomena,* and *ideas* (from the verb *idein,* "to see"). Even the verb "to say" (*femi*) has its root in *pifausko,* "to illuminate."

Truth, then, for the Greeks was "that which was commonly apparent to all:"[vii] the experience of epistemic disclosure, of a relationship possessing *logos*. Sensible disclosure is given to everyone, while *logos*-possessing relationships (the adoption of formational *logos*) are experienced individually. So what assurance do we have that our individual relational experiences with a phenomenon that is common to all conveys to us true (unhidden) knowledge, accurate (not-inaccurate) *logos*, and realistic (non-illusory) experience?

This question was answered early (in the sixth century BC) and once again by Heraclitus: "We speak the truth in what we share in common, and we are deceived in what we know on our own."[viii] Knowledge is true (verified) when it is shared in common. To say "I share in common" means that I am in tune (my experiences coincide) with the epistemic results of the experiential relationships that all my fellow human beings have with the same physical existent or event. All those who verify critically (by judging and comparing) that their recognition of an existent or event before them converges avoid "knowing on their own"—they do not have their "own *logos*" (with everyone having a different epistemic relationship). "Everyone is of the same opinion and testifies to it individually."

In the fifth century, Democritus provided an example of how verification functions in relation to sweet and sour taste. If someone maintained in company that honey is sour, those present who had tasted honey (those who had a firsthand experience of tasting honey) would object, with the certitude of experience, that honey is sweet. Experiential verification is the only criterion by which to judge who speaks the truth ("the criterion of truth") and who is mistaken. If all, or a majority, affirm, on the basis of their participatory experience of taste, that honey is sweet (if the sweetness of honey is commonly shared by whoever tastes it), then the claim of sweetness is true and that of sourness false. Truth is the affirmation of what is commonly shared by experience (what is common and converges with the experience of all or a majority) and falsehood is the unshared fixation on one's own private wisdom (individual thought, perception, and arrogant opinion that is not commonly

---

vi Translator's note: *kata-noisi*: Yannaras places a hyphen in the Greek word for "understanding/comprehension/apprehension" in order to emphasize its etymological sense of "according to the intellect."
vii Heraclitus, *Die Fragmente der Vorsokratiker*, 148, 22.
viii Ibid., 148, 24–35.

shared). Words (the signifiers of experience) are true when the experience of participating in what they signify is held in common—the experience of the majority aligns with the reality signified by the signifiers.[ix]

The criterion of truth, then, is the common opinion (of all or a majority) when that opinion reflects a convergence of verified experience. Such a convergence does not standardize the discrete experiences of individuals, but simply coordinates them, leading to a common understanding of each individual experience. The human voice provides an iconic example of an epistemic participation that preserves the subjective otherness of experience, while at the same time being integrated into a common understanding: the human voice "is shared indivisibly by all in the same way that one and the same sound is perceived by numerous ears."[x]

We finish with a final word on the epistemic function of *communally shared* experience. The polysemic Greek term *logos* refers to the referentiality of every disclosure (every phenomenon), as well as the capacity to subjectively receive the appearance of what is referenced. *Logos* also means the ability to compare (critically contrast) the way that each disclosure is subjectively received, that is, whether that way converges or differs. Convergence permits *communication* (common understanding), the convergence of common receptions (of phenomena, beings, events) through *logos* bearing the same sensible representations and images of physical beings and events. "Communion"—an activity or state that creates something common, partaken in by many—is the name the Greeks gave to this participatory knowledge, to this coordinated understanding and sensible experience, to communication as common understanding and the reception of sensible (phenomenal) images received through *logos*.

[ix] "Necessity generally became man's teacher in all things." Democritus, *Die Fragmente der Vorsokratiker II*, 136, 12–13.

[x] English translation taken from Pseudo-Dionysius, "The Divine Names," in *Pseudo-Dionysius: The Complete Works*, trans. Colm Luibheid (New York: Paulist Press, 1987), 102. Adapted.

10 Politics
Contest or art?

The next step for the Greeks was the desire to participate in the mode of truth, the mode of immortality, "the mode of universal governance," the desire to organize their relations with each other according to the mold of truth and immortality—the relations of the ornamental universe according to *logos* (order and harmony). Thus was born, for the first time in human history, the *polis*, political life, political art, and political science.[i] To the Greeks, the *polis* was not an expansive settlement—it wasn't quantity (the number of residents) that differentiated the *polis* from a small town, settlement, or territory. The *polis* was a qualitative discovery or achievement, a new (and different) mode of coexistence.

As we saw earlier, human coexistence originated in instrumental, utilitarian expediency. Cohabitation was a means of sharing common needs, by coordinating the production of goods, developing exchange relations, and refining the capacity to satisfy needs. The human being is, by nature, a "political animal"[ii]—sharing its needs in common is a condition of survival. In the case of the ancient Greeks, natural need was made to conform (in realized form) with the mode of truth, the mode of analogy (reiterating *logos*), harmony, ornamentality, the universal mode of governance, i.e., immortality. The Greeks chose a participatory communion of need *according to logos*, not passively bound to necessity, but transforming necessity into an accomplishment of *logos*-possessing communion.

Along both sides of the Aegean and in the intervening archipelago there was born, for the first time in human history, the need for a *criterion* by which to

---

i Plato, *Laws*, V, 736e: "political order" & VIII, 846d: "Acquiring and preserving the public order of the *polis*"; Plato, *Protagoras*, 322C: "So that *poleis* might be ordered"; Plato, *Gorgias*, trans. and rev. W.R.M. Lamb (London: William Heinemann, 1932), 464b: "The one which has to do with the soul, I call politics" & 521d: "Who attempts the true art of politics" (Both English translations taken and adapted from Plato, *Gorgias*; and Plato, *The Statesman*, trans. and rev. W.R.M. Lamb (London: William Heinemann, 1939), 303e: "The incompatible has now been eliminated by us from the science of politics" (English translation taken from Plato, *The Statesman*).
ii Aristotle, *The Eudemian Ethics*, trans. and rev. H. Rackham (Cambridge, MA: Harvard University Press, 1952), 10, 1242a, 23.

distinguish *truth* from *falsehood*, *correct* knowledge from *incorrect* knowledge, *reliable* information and news from *inaccurate* information and news. Once it had been confirmed through experience that the criterion of truth was a question of *how*, not *what* (it was a mode: the mode of *logos*-possessing relations that establishes the universe as existent and functional), the next step was to organize collective coexistence as a struggle to realize *truth* in the *microcosm of the polis*—an ornament of *logos*-possessing relations.

The *polis* and *philosophy*, and *democracy* as *a shared contest* to realize the truth, were the products of Greek needs, in other words, the unique hierarchy of needs introduced to history by the Greeks—the need for cohabitation to be a contest for the truth, for individual participation in communion to be a contest, and for the mark of citizenship to be the honor of participating in the contest for truth.

To reiterate, what makes the *polis* a co-settlement of human beings is not the number of individuals (residents) of which it is comprised, but the goal or aim of cohabitation. There are animals which live together in groups for the sake of protecting themselves from other species which threaten them, or for the sake of making it easier to find food. In such cases, however, we speak of herds, not a conscious, *logos*-formed communion of need and existence. Even the remarkable organization of a beehive (or birds, other insects, and sea creatures) is a form of cohabitation that is the product of instinctual necessity—it facilitates survival and breeding. It is not the product of choice.

We do not always, or necessarily, recognize in every human grouping or instance of collaboration a *political* event (the result of coexistence and cooperation freely chosen). We adjust our characterization according to the goal or aim for which a grouping is formed—we speak of societies, associations, companies, joint ventures, organizations, clubs, guilds, and parties, but also of crowds, mobs, masses, swarms, hordes, gangs, factions, cliques, and rings.

On the basis of this precise differentiation of purpose, the Greeks were able to distinguish the *polis* (the *political* event, *political* communion, the *demos*, the assembly) from all other forms of human collective coexistence and cooperation. *Polis* was the name given to the mode of human collective life that aspired to realize the common aim of all coexistence (the communal sharing of need), doing so via the mode of truth: the mode of relations according to the *logos*, harmony, and order that forms the ornamental beauty of the immortal universe.

Hence, the Greeks did not regard participation in the common affairs of the *polis* as an individual right that fortified the narcissism of the ego, that is, a legally enshrined demand for individual security or the right to impose oneself. It is exceedingly difficult today, if not impossible, for us to comprehend, through our own lived experiences, that the pursuit of truth ought to take priority over utility, living as we do a globalized mode of life (civilization) manifestly centered on the individual, with the entrenched habits of an individualistic mindset and individualistic institutions and behavioral norms.

We can at least recognize (through the immediate verifying experience open to all) that there once existed a phase in human history in which truth, rather than utility, took priority, where communion assumed priority over solitude. This is not a figment of the imagination; this historical phase existed, and it bequeathed a perpetual possession which bears witness to experiences and theoretical analyses, sculptural and architectural monuments, tragedic models and the marks of institutional achievement.

Historically, the need for the priority of truth, that is, the need for truth to be identified with *participation* in a communion of experience, for *communion* to be a contest to realize an ornamental and harmonious order characterized by *logos*, survived, embodied in certain populations. This communal form of collective existence endured for centuries and has left behind certain forms of organized common life: the ancient Greek *polis* and democracy, as well as the self-governing *communities* of Byzantium within the royal order of the Greco-Roman world.[iii] The priority of communally realized truth existed in unbroken continuity from Heraclitus (sixth century BC) to the fall of Constantinople (1453).

iii Translator's note: *oikoumene*.

11 Shared need as shared truth

In a further attempt at definition, we might say that the Greeks gave the name *polis* to that mode of coexistence, cohabitation, or co-settlement that sought to realize the aim of all human collective life, that is to say, the communal sharing of need, on the understanding that its attainment required a contest, or struggle, for shared truth. In other words, the relations that constitute cohabitation (relations of production, exchange, collaboration, common defense, functional organization, the administration of justice, common sport and entertainment, religious worship, etc.) cannot not be purely utilitarian. They must be relations *according to logos*: relations aimed at balancing individual differences and ambitions modeled on the harmony and ornamental order of the universe's coexistence—the mode of immortality.

The Greeks, like all humans, were mortal by nature. Yet, in spite of their given mortality, they sought to exist by the mode of immortality—the incorruptible, immutable, and eternal mode by which the universe is governed. They longed to taste, if only ephemerally (as human life itself is) the experience of true existence. In the language and outlook of today, we might say that the Greek *polis* (the art and science of *politics*) originally had a *metaphysical* character. However, we must conceptualize metaphysics in a way that is free of any ideological religious element or character, whether individualistic a priori assumptions, irrational (emotive) mysticism, or the certitudes of a transcendent power imposed on everyone.

Metaphysics,[i] for the Greeks, meant a species or realm of knowledge and science that began where the observation, verification, and investigation of nature ended. Natural[ii] knowledge and science observe, verify, and investigate all the physical and spatiotemporal properties of existents: shape, weight, color, composition, functionality, etc. Metaphysics studies the existent purely

---

i Translator's note: *meta-fysiki*: Yannaras inserts a hyphen in the Greek word for "metaphysics" in order to emphasize the etymological sense "after nature" or "beyond nature."
ii Translator's note: *fysiki*, here best translated as "natural," but relating back to "physics" in metaphysics—the adjective *fysikos* means both "natural" and "physical" in Greek.

in respect of the characteristics of its existence—what it means for something to exist and what it means to not exist. What is the "it" that makes existents exist? What is the cause and purpose of existing? What is the relationship between existents and existing, and what is the possible distinction between the two?

The questions investigated by metaphysics have the same rational legitimacy as those investigated by physics, and therefore deserve answers with the same rational integrity as those demanded in physics. Rational integrity does not imply that such answers ought to be validated by resort to some commonly accepted *authority* or *convention* (method or agreement), but by means of the convergence, alignment, and communion of every partial (individual) experience. Something can be considered true when "everyone is of the same opinion" (they have a common opinion, perception, or critical reception of reality) and "they testify to it individually."

Indeed, when it comes to knowledge sought via physical observation and investigation, consensus is often within easy reach—there are many codes in common use capable of providing cogent proof (sensible observation, experiment, mathematical calculation). In contrast, when it comes to the interpretive proposals of metaphysics, the principal question (the cause and purpose of existents and existence) is not subject to commonly accepted (obligatory for everyone) verification.

This is because the concepts "cause" and "purpose" do not relate to the descriptive verification of what exists, but rather to an interpretation of the intentions that made the non-existent existent. In other words, the concepts "cause" and "purpose" self-evidently presuppose the existence of a *logos*-possessing conduit (which cannot be known through sensible immediacy) through which the intentions enable the existent to participate in existence. We describe this conduit as *logos*-possessing for the fact that the very concept of intentions presupposes a mode of *logos*-possessing existence and activity.

The term *logikotita* [*logos*-ness] refers to acts and their motivations in such a way that recognizes their sheer indeterminacy, in complete contrast to the way that determinism and necessity make an act's result, along with the motivation that prompted it, predictable. In the context of our sensible world, the *intention* of an act, that is, its originating *will* and its (predefined) outcome, is characteristic of human acts alone. It is beyond the scope of the present work to conduct an extensive analysis of this human uniqueness. We merely note that the key characteristic of the human being's *logos-possessing* existence is its active (indeterminate on account of will) formation of relationships with surrounding physical reality and other humans. Human beings form and actualize relationships, freely choosing associations that fulfill their needs—such associations are not self-forming.

Our common and shared experiences as human beings allow us to distinguish *intentional* acts, differentiating them from those of necessity (lacking intention and choice, i.e., deterministic), whether undertaken in the realm of the animate (in which we participate) or the inanimate. We regard intentional acts as being of higher value (representing a higher quality of life) than necessary and deterministic acts. Our preference for autonomy of will and action is primordially given; we attempt, as far as possible, to deny or avoid necessity and the demands of determinism. "Freedom" is the name we give to the potentiality of intentional action (thought, judgment, will, imagination, goals, and creation).

12 The pre-political character of freedom

Freedom is a given feature of common human experience, subject to common (shared) validation or invalidation. The realization of this experiential potential is subject to complete indeterminacy—freedom can be pursued, but it is not a predetermined fact. We comprehend that freedom is given for the human being, even though it is not existentially constant, nor closed—it is clearly capable of development, cultivation, and endless expansion, with the potential for unforeseen, unpredetermined, and completely unique choices. By the same token, we attest that freedom is an existential potential (a *mode* of existing) that precedes preferential choice, in which case it could be defined as the originating potential of intentionality, a potential not subject to any kind of necessary instinctual drives. This primordial and commonly experienced knowledge of the freedom of intentionality (its indeterminate character) provides a basis for investigating the possibility of explaining the cause and purpose of existence, notwithstanding the dilemma it creates. Either we accept that there is no *logos-possessing* (out of free intention) cause of existence, in which case both the fact of existence and the incredible multifariousness of existents would have to be attributed to the ignominy of blind (uninterpretable) chance, or we construe human *logikotita* (freedom) as an echo (icon) of the first cause of existence and existents.

The second option entails choosing an attitude towards reality, a point of epistemic access, instead of limiting ourselves to verifiable information. An analogy might be the different attitudes one can take towards a painting. As a matter of verifiable information, one could define the painting as merely consisting of a wooden frame, a canvas affixed to the frame, and colors on the canvas (watercolor, oil color, or what have you). However, our attitude towards a painting becomes relational (an epistemic event of a different order, always constituting experiential and positive knowledge) when we begin to recognize the unique, distinct, and unrepeatable character of the painting's design, the blending and mixture of its tints and hues and other similar elements of uniqueness.

Our attitude towards the painting becomes a relationship with its creator when our observation identifies in it a creative act of otherness (unique and distinct): a uniqueness that is not symptomatic of chance, but is rather a personal expression of existence. The difference in kind between these two epistemic events is immense. Observation, verification, and validation provide consistent information that is commonly accessible to all. *Relationships*, on the other hand, are unlimited in their epistemic potential—they are perpetually on the verge of completion, but never final; they are actively attainable, but never exhaustible.

13 The alignment of the *ecclesia* of the demos and the *ecclesia* of the believers

Positing the *cause* of existence as a creative *presence*, rather than irrational[i] *chance*, is the most logically and experientially coherent option because only in-*logos* presence really warrants (justifies logically) what our lived experiences bring us to call "beauty"—the *logos*-possessing mode in which reality is composed, articulated, and structured, which is to say a mode that invites relationship: "Beauty bids all things to itself, whence it is called beauty."[ii]

It is a historical fact (not merely a hypothesis) that the Greeks aspired to imitate the beauty, or "cosmos,"[iii] of the reality of the universe (*the mode of universal governance*) in the organization and operation of their collective life. This element of cosmic beauty, which attracts and invites participation, is identifiable with the mode of immortality, truth, and real existence. The Greeks, desiring immortality, organized their common life together, in other words, the *polis* or *political* coexistence, according to the mode of pursuing and realizing truth.

The *polis* was not the product of coincidence or circumstance, nor the size of cohabitation. It was the product of an active and continual achievement: the transformation of human collective life into a contest to *share* both need and the truth.

A *communion* of need is the motivation and goal of human collective life. With the division of labor, the needs of every human can be satisfied more fully and with greater ease. This also applies to the animal kingdom, to some extent. However, human cohabitation (or coexistence) differs from a beehive or an anthill insofar as it constitutes a *polis*, and it does so when the motivation and goal of sharing need in common is not merely the fulfillment of need, but the purposeful, active imitation of existence "according to truth," that is, of

---

i Translator's note: *alogi*, literally "non-*logos*."
ii Translation taken from Pseudo-Dionysius, "The Divine Names," in *Pseudo-Dionysius*, trans. Colm Luibheid, 76. Adapted.
iii Translator's note: *kosmon*, with the sense of order in classical Greek, but etymologically connected to words denoting decoration and ornament in Modern Greek, such as *kosmima* and *kosmisi*, hence the connection Yannaras draws between it and beauty (*kallos*).

DOI: 10.4324/9781003410867-14

The alignment of the ecclesia of the demos and the believers 41

relations *according to the logos* (harmony, ornamentality, and beauty) of the universe's good order.

The realization of good order according to *logos* is an achievement because the instinctive human impulse is to satisfy individual drives as a matter of priority. As Heraclitus said, "though the account is common, the many live, however, as though they had a private understanding."[iv] Accordingly, the formation and function of the *polis* is a deliberate pursuit (a political art)—it is the struggle for liberation from the deterministic necessity of individualism. And the *ecclesia of the demos* served as the iterative event through which the *political* achievement was realized and disclosed (i.e., "truth"-as-manifestation).

The scandal, however, was that the democratic *polis* was a chosen and achieved *imitation* (excellent and perfect) of given existential necessity, and not the consequence of unpredetermined existential choice. The true, which is to say, the incorruptible, the immutable, the immortal element in existential reality, was not a mode of freedom, but of necessity. Even God, the first cause of existents, was bound "by the *logos* of his essence" to be that which he *is*. His existence was inexplicably given and predetermined; he could not cease to be what he *is*.

This originating existential necessity, the enigma of what it means to exist, is probably the most important reason why the adoption of Christianity by the Greeks was completed so rapidly and in such a short time span, within approximately a century. Indeed, it occurred under conditions in which Christians faced deadly persecution from a Roman authority that sought to preserve its *religio imperii* (Emperor worship), a visible cornerstone of cohesion in the multiethnic Roman Empire.

The Greeks regarded the *Ecclesia's* good news (gospel)[v] as a triumph of freedom, as an existential possibility in contrast to blind determinism. The first cause of existence and existents was no longer a cosmic rationality without explanation—worthy of admiration, but given, like destiny. The primordial cause of existence was now understood to be an unpredetermined, *logos*-possessing, willing freedom. The conviction of this Christian experience is epitomized in the statement "God *is* love."[vi]

What does this proposition mean? It means that the cause of everything that exists itself exists because it freely *wills* to exist, and it wills to exist because it *loves*. Existence is not prior to love, as though love were either a moral or behavioral attribute of the first cause. God exists because he is

---

iv Heraclitus, *Die Fragmente der Vorsokratiker*, 151, 2. English translation taken from Heraclitus, *Fragments*.

v Translator's note: *eu-aggelio*. Yannaras inserts a hyphen to highlight the etymological meaning of "gospel," which is "good news." Subsequent instances of hyphenation are translated "gospel (good news)" in the text.

vi Translator's note: 1 John 4:16. Italics Yannaras'.

Trinitarian, that is, because he *is* love: the freedom of love *instantiates*,[vii] gives real existence to, God as a Father who begets the Son and sends forth the Spirit. The first cause of existence exists, not because it is God, which is to say compelled to be what he is by the given *logos* of his nature or essence, but because he is the *Father*: the one who instantiates his existence as freedom, which is to say love, "begetting," and "sending forth," or "creating" (in the case of material creation) instantiated existence.

The constitutive principle of Greek epistemology—"what can be shared can be verified"—clearly not only relates to distinguishing between correct and false testimony, information, or news. It also relates to *true existence*, to truth as existential fullness and freedom from every existential limitation (necessity) of space, time, corruption, and death. Access to the truth cannot therefore be equated with a correct individual understanding of reality, for this presupposes experiential (willing, free, and loving) *participation* in surrounding reality. Only *love* is capable of producing knowledge (and truth), that is, the dynamic existential freedom of relationship, not individual understanding, verification, or attestation,

In principle, we define "relationship" as an event of freedom. It is not something self-evidently and necessarily given, nor a product or result of a given (natural) operation, such as intellect, imagination, intuition, or something else. Relationship is that epistemic access to reality that is realized as a form of freedom from all necessity, and therefore from all expediency. To say that "I relate" to something is to say that I seek to know it, not for the sake of using it or profiting from it (to place it in the service of my individual needs or desires), but to know it purely for what it *is* and for why it *is*. Relationships presuppose our liberation and freedom from the innate (deterministic) necessities of selfishness from which our physical existence suffers—necessities are passions of our nature (passions of self-preservation, supremacy, and pleasure).

Relationships, on the other hand, as a function of freedom, vary in terms of their quality along a broad spectrum, in the same way that freedom can be achieved to a greater or lesser extent. If love is the fullest realization of freedom, then clearly the fullest and most complete relationships are those that are loving. Love equates to the fullest epistemic relationship, that is, the fulfillment of knowledge.

---

vii Translator's note: *ypostasiazei*, literally *"hypostasize."*

14 The exercise of authority as responsible service

During the centuries of the Greek paradigm, the concept "*ecclesia* of the demos" referred to the achievement of the *polis*: the struggle to transcend individual drives so that collective life could attain the *logos*-possessing harmony, order, and ornamentality of the truth (according to necessity) of the universe. And in the Christian continuity of the Greek paradigm, the word *ecclesia* referred to the matter of self-transcendence, that self-transcendence which realizes freedom as an existential relational communion of love—an icon of the Trinitarian first cause of existence.

The contest of communal self-transcendence, which is to say the Christian *Ecclesia*, did not generate, in the context of the Greek paradigm, a specific and intended collective constitutional form—a form analogous (or different or antithetical) to ancient Greek democracy or the Jewish monarchy, or any other kind. Indeed, the noun *ecclesia* clearly reflected what was signified by the term "democracy": an *Ecclesia* was the result of "calling out,"[i] the event of "calling" or convening an assembly[ii] (co-presence) comprising the totality of citizens (the demos) which administered authority (*power*).[iii] Democracy[iv] connoted the possession of power[v] by the whole demos (it ruled and exercised authority)—the entire citizenry and the *ecclesia* of the demos were the true manifestation of this *mode*-event.

(Nouns,[vi] in the understanding of the Greeks, signified a mode of existence that could be known only through the experience of participation. Nouns

---

i Translator's note: *ek-kalein*. A reference to the etymology of the noun *ecclesia*, which literally means "calling out."
ii Translator's note: Yannaras hyphenates the Greek word for assembly (*syn-eleusi*) to highlight the etymological sense of "coming together."
iii Translator's note: *kratos*. An allusion to the second component in the Greek word "democracy" (*dimokratia*), and thus relating to the earlier reference to "demos," the first component in "democracy."
iv Translator's note: *dimo-kratia*, hyphenated to highlight the etymological sense of "people-power."
v Translator's note: *kratei*, the verbal form of the noun *kratos*, referring back to *kratia* in *dimokratia* (demo*cracy*).
vi Translator's note: *onomata*, also "names."

DOI: 10.4324/9781003410867-15

denoted, disclosed, and conveyed the truth (unhiddenness) of each existent, that is, the distinct mode in which it participated in being. They thus referred to an existent's essence because as Plato said, "we ourselves say of that which partakes of essence that 'it is.'"[vii] A noun did not refer to an ontic monad (a singular entity), but to the singularity of a mode ("identity of definition and of constituent characteristics establishes a type of unity" which "denotes the essence").[viii] Today, in the context of our modern paradigm, it is difficult to comprehend an epistemic function whereby nouns refer to the indeterminacy of relationships rather than to the delimitation of entities. There exist, of course, words that recapitulate relationships, which do not refer to static facts, but rather to a single common factor (or field) of actualized relation (father, brother, homeland, public festival). Comprehension of terms such as these differs very clearly from the comprehension of concepts that define the common properties of entities (tall, short, heavy, light, fast, slow, etc.) Nouns have a single point of reference, but knowledge of them presupposes a recapitulatory experience of relationships, whereas the definitions of common qualities presuppose intellectual (individual) comprehension of concepts that are quantifiable (height, weight, speed, etc.).

Democracy, then, in the context of the Greek paradigm, did not signify something consummated, but rather a means of moving towards a goal, the challenge of achieving something, premised on the dynamic (and indeterminate) relations of shared life. The word "democracy" did not refer to constants reified in institutional form, to a final form of collective life along predetermined lines. On the contrary, it signified an evolving[ix] "shared contest" aimed at transforming the communion of need into a real communion of truth. Common need set the goal, not a programmatic decision—it was the will of the citizens to establish their coexistence and cohabitation as the mode of truth, that is, immortality: "the mode of universal governance."

The word "democracy" connoted dynamic relations, exactly in the way that words like "father," "chorus," "public festival" or "homeland," connote relationships. None of these words (nor others like them) connote or certify something necessary, exhortatory, prescriptive, or obligatory (an instrumental-utilitarian imperative), nor in any way submission to organizational, functional, or behavioral constants. They refer to signifieds that are ontological, not deontological.

---

vii Plato, *Cratylus*, trans. and rev. H.N. Fowler (Cambridge, MA: Harvard University Press, 1939), 401c, 6–7. Adapted.
viii Aristotle, *The Physics*, rev. trans. Philip H. Wicksteed and Francis M. Cornford (London: William Heinemann, 1957), I.185b, 7–8. English translation taken from Aristotle, *The Physics*; Aristotle, *The Metaphysics*, trans. Hugh Tredennick (London: William Heinemann, 1933), VII.1028a, 13–5. Adapted; Christos Yannaras, *The Schism in Philosophy: The Hellenic Perspective and Its Western Reversal*, trans. Norman Russell (Brookline, MA: Holy Cross Orthodox Press, 2015), Chapter 14.
ix Translator's note: *gignomeno*, literally "becoming."

In the context of today's fixed and all-encompassing individualistic civilizational paradigm, we primarily (or exclusively) understand the meaning of signifiers intellectually; we do not recall the lived experiences of having participated in *modes*. We therefore find it difficult, if not impossible, to discern with any clarity the epistemic difference between the ontological and deontological versions of democracy. We exclusively understand the words "democracy" and "*ecclesia*" (of the demos) as the perceived achievements of equality before the law and equal citizenship, and even then, as something from the distant past, in which case democracy can only be understood deontologically, merely as an ideal goal containing the normative principles of an ideology.

The ontological version of democracy preserves the epistemic clarity that comes from need, while the deontological preserves the clarity of concepts that can be mastered by the individual human mind. The necessary [*deon*] in the deontological version (the appropriate or obligatory) has been predetermined by someone on the rationalistic (to the extent possible) grounds of common utility. In the ontological perspective, democracy emerges from the need to realize and manifest being, and being together according to truth, whereas in the deontological version democracy is a matter of utility (the best of its kind).

15 The common roots of democracy, community, and the parish

The ontological version of democracy, with existential truth as its common goal, was a historical reality, albeit for a short period of time, in the ancient Greek *polis*. The purpose of the *polis* could be seen clearly in philosophical discourse, tragedian iconology, and the language of architecture and sculpture. The communal pursuit of what is true continued in the self-governing community parishes (an organic extension of the Christian Eucharistic gathering) in the period of the Greco-Roman world, as well as in the dark days of the Ottoman period.

On what basis can we verify the continuity of the Greek *polis*, the struggle of *democracy*, in the ecclesial community of the Eucharistic parish? The first basis is the absence in both cases of an ideological agenda arising from intellection: beliefs, i.e., the desire to achieve utility. The *polis* and the *parish community* both emerged from the maturation of common need, the need for common life to be true, to manifest *according to truth*. And *true* existence (free from limitation and necessity) is worthy in its own right—its pursuit needs no further justification, nor any reward.

Utility was not a preeminent concern in the Greek *polis* and the ecclesial *parish community*, at either the organizational or functional levels. Nor was a *legal* framework that sought to secure a mode of coexistence based on efficacy. There is no need, therefore, to glamorize this mode with idealistic rhetoric, nor to conflate utility with benevolence using psychological constructs.

The junctions that provided the continuity (and sense of time) in Greek collective life were the festal cycles: paschal, annual, and weekly. The feast served as the axis around which the society-community cohered (as opposed to some contract or convergence of principles, rules, or values). The requirements of Greek continuity and cohesion were not preset deontologically. They were born of common and shared *need*, and the standard by which that need was assessed and evaluated was the plenitude of festal communion.

An accurate illustration would be to liken the feast to the warp that weaves the woof of (civilizational) continuity and social cohesion, continually embodying the meaning of existence in a mode of life, a continuity of

DOI: 10.4324/9781003410867-16

"excellent and perfect action."[i] The excellent and perfect action of the Greek mode finds its continuity in philosophical discourse, architecture, sculpture, icons, music, and institutions.

In the context of today's individualistic civilizational paradigm, we primarily understand in terms of concepts and intellectual constructs; rarely, and then only deficiently, do we participate experientially in a *mode*. We mainly have individual (chosen) beliefs, not verifying experiences. Truth is not the criterion by which we evaluate; utility alone is. Thus, the quest for utility quickly descends into an effort to win over impressions, to paper over the clash of interests.

It is difficult in the context of this individualistic paradigm to *know* (and not just comprehend) the aim of the Greek *polis* and *politics*, and the Christian goal of *ecclesial* communion—to aim at fulfilling a version of existence as freedom, where freedom means self-transcendence and self-offering. It is difficult, perhaps even impossible, to know empirical facts merely through intellectual analysis and the coherent articulation of logical propositions. Restricting the epistemic field solely to the way physical and historical change appears does not lead to knowledge. In the context of today's dominant global paradigm of historical-materialism, human life is treated purely as though it were a product of the relations of production, exchange, and consumption, and existence as though it were purely a meaningless process of survival defined by contracts that secure rights, which is to say, the freedom of choice.

In any event, the immeasurable gulf that today separates European societies from everything they pretend to admire without reservation, namely ancient Greek democracy and the early Christian *Eclessia*, presents a challenge for those societies, even if they are not aware of it. The problem is not a paucity of information; it is the lack of access to knowledge as relational experience, to freedom as an experience of self-transcendence and to existence as a shared event. It is rather perplexing that the post-Roman West fell into the trap of perverting democracy into a representative system. The function of politics became steeped in the crutches of ideology and the expediency of utilitarianism, in the same way that the ecclesial event became ensnared in the formalism of a religiosity that is, by definition, individualistic. These pitfalls are painful and disorientating, but also revealing. They illuminate, *a contrario*, important facets of the human condition.

---

i Aristotle, *Poetics*, trans. and with a commentary. George Whalley (Montreal: McGill-Queen's University Press, 1997), 1449b21.

16 The political consequences of the *Ecclesia's* religionization

Today we define the term Europe semantically and experientially as a historical reality that emerged between the fourth and sixth centuries AD in the central, western, and northern part of the continent. The population changes that occurred in these locations during this period formed a cosmogonic (in the literal sense) event: the invasion and settlement of barbarian (i.e., at a primitive stage of development) tribes and races, and the attendant disruption and marginalization (or indeed extermination) of native populations. This resulted in a radical civilizational change, the most consequential to date in human history.

These changes did not merely undermine the level of cultivation and the manifold development of Europe at the time; they also transformed and reconstituted collective organization and function in a manner that was historically unprecedented. The invader-colonists coveted the remarkable achievements of the Greco-Roman world (for that age). But above all, perhaps even exclusively, they were impressed by the level of prosperity and the practical conveniences of life offered by that world.

At the time, there was a widely entrenched conviction that Christianity was the key factor of civilization, that is, of an advanced life. While this was true, the mistake made by the invader-settlers (perhaps unavoidable) was to regard Christianity as a religion, one clearly superior to their own pagan and mythological religions, but a religion nonetheless, with infallible doctrines, obligatory rules, and guaranteed promises. Christianity was not understood as an *ecclesia*, a truth won solely through communally shared, experiential participation, a *mode* of existence rather than merely a mode of behavior. Everyone and anyone could embrace Christianity as a form of superior religion, centered on the individual, as all religions are, as a means of gaining access to the incredible achievements of the societies of the Greco-Roman world.

In other words, the invader-settlers thought that the prerequisite for their desired equal participation in the good life—on equal terms with the other peoples of the *imperium romanum*—was simply to change religion. And how is one inducted into Christianity? Through baptism. So the barbarians were baptized *en masse* in rivers and lakes (often obeying the commands of their

DOI: 10.4324/9781003410867-17

leaders who had the right to make decisions for them). They conformed to the institutional forms and rhetoric of church practice, unaware of the leap required to transition from the individualism of religion to the shared existence of membership in the *ecclesia*.

It is worth reiterating and highlighting the prolonged ignorance of the post-Roman West regarding the definitive (by definition) distinction between the Christian *Ecclesia* and the phenomenon of religion innate to human nature. Religion is indelibly individualistic in character—it presupposes individual beliefs and individual obedience to moral precepts with a view to individual salvation. Every religion is self-evidently constituted by axiomatic principles that explain the existent and determine (direct) individual behavior. The religious individual subjects himself to these principles in the psychological self-assurance that his subjection will be rewarded. He anticipates recompense following death—the extension of his existence in linear time in conditions of blissful serenity and well-being.

Ecclesia is a Greek word with a referent that is the exact opposite of religious individualism. It means or denotes the result of calling out (a call to relationship): a meeting or gathering, the event and experience of coming together or coexisting. The purpose of meeting and gathering in both the Greek *ecclesia of the demos* and the Christian *ecclesia of the faithful* was not utilitarian. The purpose of gathering was not simply to discuss problems, exchange ideas, opinions, preferences, and make decisions. In both the Greek and Christian cases, the very act of coming together in the *ecclesia* was the goal—the realization and manifestation of a *mode* of existence and coexistence, a mode "according to truth," which is to say an existence that is eternal, immutable, and incorruptible. For the Greeks, "according to truth" meant a mode of existence according to the relational *logos*, order, and harmony of the universe's ornamental beauty. For Christians, it meant relationships of *loving* self-transcendence and self-offering, of complete love, in other words, relationships free from all necessity. And such relationships were realized as a *mode* of existence through their manifestation in the historical event of the incarnation of God-*Logos*.

17 Religious totalitarianism

This *ecclesial* version of existence, truth, and divinity is completely absent from the religionized Christianity adopted by the barbarian tribes that invaded and settled the post-Roman West. All our sources (of every kind) collectively testify to and verify this absence—written sources, works of art, institutional arrangements, collective forms, and popular customs and practices.

Indeed, it is widely recognized (by researchers and historians) that one source and causal factor in the transformation of the ecclesial event into a religion in the post-Roman West, along with the primitiveness of its settlers, proved to be the writings of one of its native sons: Augustine. This indicates that the transformation of the *ecclesia* into a religion did not occur merely out of a lack of cultivation. Rather, it was a transformation symptomatic of the kind of individualistic dispositions and demands that are to be found at all levels of development, learning, and sensibility. The transformation of ecclesial truth into a religion is a potential inherent in the human impulse towards individual self-sufficiency, power, sovereignty, and coercion.

We can trace the progressive development of religious totalitarianism as a political phenomenon, as well as the militant exclusion of metaphysics from the domain of power relations, in the historical evolution of the invader-settlers in the post-Roman West (which researchers call "the Barbarian West"). "Religious totalitarianism" describes the phenomenon of coercive control, that is, policing obligatory beliefs and normative rules, as well as punishing disobedience—not just disobedience in respect of behavior (in deed), but also in respect of conscience, opinion, and expression.

Totalitarianism arose from the historical need for discipline among the primitive barbarian tribes which had invaded Europe and the arbitrary rule of their warrior leaders. All were to obey a single absolute authority on account of that authority's metaphysical prestige, namely the bishop of Rome, who sought authority for this very reason, and who with puerile ruses and historical forgeries set himself up as "God's representative on earth" (*vicarius Christi*) with absolute administrative authority over whether people received eternal salvation or eternal punishment.

DOI: 10.4324/9781003410867-18

Religious totalitarianism 51

The phenomenon of totalitarian authority, as well as the practices and methods by which it was imposed, gave birth to a new epoch in the history of politics: the infallibility of the supreme authority, the prohibition of dissent, the ultimate penalty (death by fire) for wrong worship, censorship (*index librorum prohibitorum*), systematic mass brain washing (*propaganda fidei*), and more. These practices generated the need for political efficacy by any means necessary (the ends justify the means), an authority to determine what was correct and appropriate for the collective as a whole, and the inclusion of religious considerations in the deontological aims of the exercise of authority.

The medieval experience drove modern Europe to an independent theory and practice of politics militantly divorced from all metaphysical authority, from the institutionalized forms of religiosity, and from any contemplation of the metaphysical *meaning* of human existence and coexistence. According to Böckenförde, Europe sought and achieved the following:

- The liberation of politics from all spiritual-religious determination;
- The genesis of a modern state founded on the separation of the Christian religion from all other religions;
- The desacralization of the domain of politics by dislodging the political class from the sphere of the sacred and mystical, freeing politics to pursue its own independent course;
- The cessation of the constitutional rationale of the state (organized human coexistence) being determined and oriented by faith (metaphysical objectives) and its replacement by the autonomous, individualistic, self-justifying rationale of utilitarianism;
- The expansion of religious freedom to include a citizen's right to belong to no religion at all;
- The functioning of the state in the exclusive service of worldly ends and common (organized) interests; and
- The state's obligation to guarantee its citizens' expectations of happiness.

18 Ideology
The alienation of truth into accuracy

The cosmogonic separation of politics from religion in post-medieval Europe (and beyond) did not extinguish the nightmare of totalitarianism from human history. In practice, totalitarianism proves to be a consequence not only of the absolute authority (infallibility) demanded by religious dogma, but also of the dogmatic character (the demands for blind faith) of various socio-political ideologies.

Ideology names the totality of interpretative (of reality) and normative (regarding human life) proposals derived from the work of a philosopher, social scientist, or more broadly, a school. All ideologies are prone to pretentions of authority and infallibility and are therefore susceptible to autocracy, for obvious reasons—a relatively modest evaluation of the significance (value) of such proposals would undermine the faith that inspires and animates efforts to implement them.

We must not forget that the phenomenon of ideology emerged historically from the effort or need to replace the Pope's absolute authority to represent and interpret the word of God. In sixteenth century Europe, the Protestant Reformation (*Protestatio-Reformatio*) sought to transfer the guarantees offered by the bishop of Rome's infallible pronouncements (as the "successor of Peter" and "vicar of God on Earth") to the validity of the very written word of the incarnate God (*sola scriptura*), a written word accessible to all.

This transfer preserved all of the motives that had led to the imposition of papal infallibility: the need for the religious leadership to bolster its authority with the greatest possible prestige (supernatural and divine), the practical-utilitarian need for an authority imposed on everyone as a means of securing social cohesion, and the need for valid moral norms and moral codes. Finally, there was the psychological need within every individual for the moral rules that govern their behavior and life to be of unimpeachable authority.

Recourse to the supreme authority of God's *word* (codified in written texts, no less) can avoid the autocracy and inevitable capriciousness of monarchic authority, the God-given rule of one man. But the divine *word*, in spite of being definitively articulated in written form, is still liable to a multiplicity of interpretations—the number in pursuit of the correct (authentic) interpretation is unavoidably large. This phenomenon particularly applies whenever and wherever truth is equated with accuracy instead of being the outcome of a convergence of shared experience ("when everyone is of the same opinion and testifies to it individually"). This is true of the post-Roman societies of the West.

Who possesses the most correct interpretation of the word of God in its received written from? This is to ask who the successor to papal authority is, given there have inevitably been many candidates from the outset, such as Luther, Calvin, and Zwingli. The candidates have multiplied over two centuries and now number in the hundreds. The question of accuracy ought to have been determined by objective criteria, but objectivity in this context is determined by a plethora of divergent criteria. For our purposes, what is of interest is that in the context of the Western paradigm, the demand for a successor to papal authority served as the womb that gave birth to multifarious succession attempts, some aware, others unaware, of their organic provenance and consequence. Ideologies are what we today call all these attempts to substitute the religious (metaphysical) version of infallibility with proposals which, while identical in what they demand, have been purified from metaphysical authority. Ideologies replace the esteem of the transcendence with the irresistible logic of utilitarian efficacy.

All ideologies consistently replicate the Vatican model of infallible (papal) authority. They offer certainty as a means of fortifying the ego, the validity of which is not supported by transcendent sacredness, but by the earthly utility of common logic and the additional prestige of a personality possessing unique capabilities: a Marx, Lenin, Mao, Freud, Bakunin, or Adam Smith. Adherence to an ideology (whether by choice or coercion) presupposes individual faith in the accuracy (infallibility) of the positions of its founder and a psychological commitment to the demands imposed by that faith.

Ideologies cannot function without axiomatic explanatory and normative propositions, and therefore without the self-evident need to impose their dogmas and morality, which is why the effects generated in the climate of papal absolutism are mirrored, more or less, in all ideological systems: propaganda, censorship of thought, the imperative of obedience, and the outlawing of critical thought and debate. The phenomenon (nightmare) of totalitarianism is a common consequence of the medieval and post-medieval Western European paradigm—the product of religionized, rather than *ecclesial*, Christianity.

In short, totalitarianism is the child of individualism—an overriding concern for the objective security of the individual imposed on everyone. The one and only meaning of the Greek word communion (the individual self-transcendence that is a prerequisite for *participation* in the act of communing, in the freedom of cooperation and active coexistence) precludes any accommodation with forced obedience to an instrumentally predetermined conception of the good.

19 *Societas*

The alienation of communion into partnership

It is abundantly clear that a study of the phenomenon of secularization, which is to say, a study of the historical processes that led to the liberation of politics from the control (or influence) of religious institutions in the West, is insufficient for understanding the evolution of the concepts "state" and "authority" (the collective forms and practices they signify) in so-called modernity. Secularization presupposes, and follows, changes in the *mindset* (way of thinking[i]), understanding, and sense (purpose, intentionality) of linguistic concepts and political vocabulary.

The Greek word "communion" denoted the act-event and result of "communing."[ii] "To commune" meant to do something in common with someone else or with others, leading to the acquisition of knowledge through participation by virtue of partaking in the same experience and knowledge. In Latin, the noun *societas* and the verb *socio* were the semantic analogues to the Greek "communion" and "commune." Today, the primary definition of *societas* one finds in dictionaries is "a partnership on the basis of common interest." The question of interest and mutual advantage takes precedence over any other consideration or goal. In French, the term *société anonyme* (limited liability company) openly identifies the word *societas* with business-economic cooperation, the alignment of self-interest via contract.

The Greek word for "relationship" means a reference between two or more, affinity, analogy, resemblance, connection, interdependence, close acquaintance, or a bond of friendship and love.[iii] Given that instinctive drives are

---

i Translator's note: *tropo-tou-noein*: literal translation and an allusion to the etymology of the Greek noun *nootropia* (mindset).
ii Translator's note: *koinonein*. This is the verb translated throughout as "communally share" or "share in common," here rendered as "communing" in order to retain the semantic connection to the noun *koinonia*. It is also important to note in the context of this chapter that *koinonia* is also the Modern Greek term for "society," which explains why Yannaras relates it to the Latin word *societas*.
iii Translator's note: Modern Greek does not make the distinction English does between the words "relationship" and "relation." Because "relationship" can be used interchangeably for "relation" in many instances, the term "relationship" is used to translate the Greek term *shesi/eis* throughout, except in those rare instances where "relation" makes better sense.

DOI: 10.4324/9781003410867-20

inexorably individualistic, forming a relationship presupposes the attainment of freedom from natural impulses. As an event, a relationship entails voluntary coexistence, cooperation, collaboration, communication, and counsel—one forms a relationship when one freely relinquishes individual self-sufficiency, self-complacency, self-autonomy, self-knowledge, self-determination, and self-empowerment. A relationship is not simply a form of behavior; it constitutes an existential event, a way of existing, and an achievement of freedom from egocentric impulses and the necessities which deterministically govern nature. As an achievement of freedom, however, relationships are always accompanied by the possibility of non-achievement, that is, failure. As such, all relationships involve risk and are a contest of freedom. When the maturity required to appreciate freedom is lacking, the risk inherent in relationships becomes muted or is evaded by either adhering to a normative conception of relations in terms of accuracy or by reliance on the security of a treaty or contract.[iv]

The word "truth" (*alitheia*—a compound of the privative "*a*" and "*lithi*," which did not originally mean "forgetfulness,"[v] but rather "obscurity," "non-appearance," and "hiddenness"), referred to unhiddenness, and thus to appearance, disclosure, and manifest presence. Thus "truth" was identified semantically with illumination—a thing or event "is true" when it is illuminated, when it comes into the light and becomes empirically evident to all. Illumination is identical to empirical knowledge, which is commonly accessible to all. The modern understanding of the word "truth," however, has retained, almost exclusively, the semantic content of the Latin word *veritas* and, more specifically, the content given to this Latin term originally by Anselm of Canterbury, and decisively by Thomas Aquinas: *veritas est adaequatio rei et intellectus* (truth is a correspondence between a thing and its concept-understanding). This formulation defines truth exclusively in terms of individual understanding, the offspring of the capacity of individual minds, thus excluding relationship (the communion of experience) as the path or way to truth as communally verified knowledge. It equates truth with accurate comprehension (*rectitudo sola mente perceptibilis*), whereby accuracy is secured by resort to either an *authority* or an *agreement-convention*. Individual-centered knowledge, the exclusion of communal experience, and equating truth with correct understanding and accuracy with the imposing prestige of an authority or convention, provided the framework for a new cultural paradigm diametrically opposed to the Greek paradigm.

The genuine opposition between the Greek communion-centered paradigm and the modern individual-centered paradigm is further reinforced by

---

iv Translator's note: *symvasi*—also "convention."
v Translator's note: the meaning of *lithi* in Modern Greek.

the distinct semantic content given to the word "freedom" in modernity. In the Greek tradition, freedom was identified with the unfettered, unimpeded, and voluntary action of human will—the independent, self-determining, frank, and fearlessness thought and decision-making of human beings. However, such expressions of freedom were grounded principally in the sovereign will, the requisite victory over impulsive, instinctive, irrational, and passionate drives, weakness of will, and the suppression of self-autonomy. "Slave and free are distinguished on the basis of virtue and vice," Aristotle concluded, encapsulating the Greek tradition.[vi] In complete contrast to this tradition, modernity understands and institutionalizes freedom as the individual right to unrestricted and unhindered choice.

---

vi Aristotle, *The Politics*, 1255a.40.

20 Religious "salvation" and political individualism

The civilization, or paradigm, of modernity has characteristics akin to human adolescence. In adolescence, the human being's foremost need is self-assurance. The adolescent needs to be free of adult supervision, to question certainties guaranteed on the basis of authority, and to determine truth and falsehood, good and evil, what is necessary and what is optional on the basis of individual experience.

The contemporary international paradigm of modernity emerged in Western Europe, which is to say in societies in which modernity, as it is known today, succeeded many centuries of civilizational infancy and underdeveloped civilizational imitation. The peoples that now make up the societies of Western Europe, currently the envy of the world, entered the historical and civilizational scene when they invaded the territories of the Western Roman Empire between the fourth and sixth centuries AD. The centuries in which they moved through civilizational infancy (the middle ages: between barbarism and civilization) have been the subject of rigorous study—the relevant literature is detailed and vast.

Hellenism and Christianity played the role of guardians during the Western settlers' journey towards maturity. The Latin cultural tradition of Old Rome began to recede (at least, outwardly) in 476 AD when the German Odoacer deposed Romulus Augustulus, the last Latin Emperor of the Roman West. Old Rome's cultural influence came to an eventual end in the West (manifestly) when German bishops acceded to the papal throne (from the eighth century).

The neophyte West's teenage resistance to its guardians, Hellenism and Christianity, came in the form (as it so often does in the case of the psychology of the individual) of both an aggressive rejection and an attempt at exclusive misappropriation. As long as Hellenism was still active in the march of history (until the fall of the New Rome, Constantinople, in 1453 at the hands of the Ottomans), Europe's newcomers, keen for their political autonomy, sought to establish a second empire in the West: the Holy Roman Empire of the German Nation. The notion of an "empire," first embodied in human history by the Romans, constituted an "order of things" (*ordo rerum*) in the international realm and not simply a scheme or form of authority. This "order of things"

DOI: 10.4324/9781003410867-21

molded a *way of life* or culture that in many respects preserved the Roman Empire's internal Hellenization—the Greek historical embodiment received by Christianity through its adoption of the language and tradition of Greek philosophy. The civilizational foundation established by the German empire differed from the Greek empire, and as such presupposed a different *religio imperii*.

From the ninth century in particular, the barbarian West, then fragmented into kingdoms and principalities, aspired to religious unity, whether naturally and unconsciously or consciously and deliberately, as a means of gaining autonomy from the unified body of the Christian world—from both the one universal church and the Roman "order of things." There are many factors that brought about this historical development, and they have been studied from many perspectives. The verdict, however, is beyond dispute and all too clear: such a differentiation could not have occurred (and manifested so emphatically) without innovations in the teaching and witness of both the West's ecclesial experience and practice of ecclesial life.

At the same time that a deliberate effort of differentiation was at work, an aggressive attempt at exclusive misappropriation was also in operation. This was the preposterous fiction that the post-Roman barbarian West had assumed the mantle of ancient Greek (classical) tradition, which began to appear in the West during the so-called early Renaissance of the twelfth century (with the first translation of Aristotle's *Organon*). Christianized Hellenism was supposed to have abandoned this mantle with Justinian's landmark closure (a symbolic gesture) of the last philosophical schools in Athens in 529 AD!

Setting aside the problem of chronological fabrications, what did it mean in practice for the neophyte West to aggressively reject its guardians, Hellenism and Christianity? The West read (and reads) ancient Greek tradition in its own *way*, whether texts, institutions, art, or practices. The difference between the Western and Greek readings can be encapsulated in their construals of the word "truth" (unhidden). For the Greeks, "truth" always meant "unhidden," which is to say apparent, manifest, illuminated, and therefore *experientially* knowable, open to *shared* knowledge, to the experience of *participation* in the object of knowledge through a *relationship* with it.

For the West, "truth" meant *correct*—the opposite of false, mistaken, or unreliable. Yet, the experience of *participation* in seeing or observing what is true is judged to be reliable when testimonies to the experience converge and are shared: "We speak the truth in what we share, but we are deceived in what we know on our own."[i] In contrast, confirmation that something is *correct* presupposes an external empirical *authority* that is imposed on everyone, or a voluntary contract or convention, which is also imposed on everyone who is a party to the contract.

---

i Heraclitus, *Die Fragmente der Vorsokratiker I*, 148, 29–30.

Religious "salvation" and political individualism

From the outset, there have been (and will always be) two divergent and incompatible versions of "truth." On the one hand, there is the Greek version of truth as *participatory* knowledge and certainty through *shared* experience. On the other hand, there is the Western version of truth as individual intellectual understanding, guaranteed by the force of an infallible *authority*, in the form of either an institution or convention. These two radically antithetical and, by definition, irreconcilable versions of truth stem from (or perhaps institute or constitute—likely both, historically) a wider, more general stance of life: communion-centered and individual-centered. And by "stance of life," is meant a developed and practical (collectively established) choice of priorities, or evaluation of priorities, in which the priority is either the joy and trust of a *relational communion* or the certitude of a secured and fortified *ego*.

The fundamental factor (or primary reason) that led to the genesis and development of the individual-centered stance is, manifestly, the innately given natural (instinctive) urges of *self-preservation, domination-sovereignty*, and *pleasure*. Existence as survival has never been optional for the human being; it is a response to given *urges*, which is to say necessity. In the perspective (and language) of ecclesial experience, however, the individual-centered *mode* of existence only determines and demarcates *created* existences, whereas the kind of existence that is instituted and actualized as freedom of love is the mode of the uncreated. The human being possesses a given capacity for *volition*, that is, the potential to be free from the instinctive urges of its created individualism: the human being has access to a *mode* of existence "after the likeness"[ii] of the uncreated, existence as the freedom of self-transcendence and self-offering.

Freedom from the instinctive necessities (urges) of individualism presupposes active will, practical effort, and arduous and difficult resistance to the human being's very own nature, which is to say resistance to the deterministically given *mode* of createdness. This is why every collective (organized) human effort to exist in a way that transforms coexistence into a common struggle—to be free from the determinism of individualism and to exist according to the priority of shared knowledge rather than individual knowledge[iii]—is deemed to be a superior, more honorable, and enviable *mode* of existence. The Greek *polis* and the early Christian *ecclesial community* provide indicative historical examples (the highest examples) of standards or models where the priority of communion was a reality, where communion was identified with the truth.[iv]

---

ii Translator's note: the language is taken from Gen. 1:26 in the Septuagint.

iii Translator's note: the language here refers back to the Heraclitus quote above: "We speak the truth in what we share, but we are deceived in what we know on our own." This is evident in the Modern Greek text by Yannaras' use of terms from the Heraclitus quote in their ancient Greek form.

iv Translator's note: again, the language refers back to the Heraclitus quote above.

21 Materialistic and idealistic utilitarianism

The Greek democratic *polis* and the Christian *ecclesial* community did not function (nor do they function today) as ideal historical types, in the sense of either a formula or optimum goal. Rather, their principal function was to illuminate the most important question in the dynamic realm of human relationships. True love can never assume the character of a moral imperative, nor an instrumental norm or ideological goal. Love is largely an achievement of undetermined factors, an achievement that primarily illuminates and evaluates every other event of love. The same goes for the Greek democratic *polis* and the Christian *ecclesial* community: they illuminate and evaluate all other political events.

It is difficult to explain why *democracy* and the *ecclesia* both came to be exploited historically—the promotion (and often imposition) of corruption, falsification, and the alienation of a once genuine and authentically realized achievement. What we know as democracies today amount to regimes and polities constituted and organized on the basis of a blatant rejection of the foundational characteristics of the original event, resulting in institutional forms which, in the best-case scenario, are concerned with protecting individual rights, rights that prioritize and grant autonomy to the ego, and which secure unrestrained self-interest.

In a similar vein, the term *ecclesia* is today applied to collective forms of individualistic religiosity, where the pursuit of individual salvation via accomplishments that earn individual reward is predominant (obeying the legal requirements of orthodoxy and orthopraxy). In other words, the meaning of *ecclesia* has come to be identified with its complete antithesis, religion, and thus identifiable with all of the effects that typically flow from collective expressions of individualism, such as ideological conscription, factional discipline, militant piety, intellectual propaganda, and the esotericism of emotions.

History shows rather clearly that the forms in which human collective life are organized and function emerge from (or reflect) the interpretations (the meaning) we attribute to natural reality as it is given to us humans (to the environment of our existence). The inability or refusal to attribute meaning (cause and purpose) to natural reality logically leads to the embrace of *chance*

DOI: 10.4324/9781003410867-22

(i.e., irrationality[i]) as the principal cause of the real and the existent, in which case it follows that satisfying instinctive demands and appetites is an absolute priority. However, restraining this priority for the purposes of the utilitarian satisfaction of the needs of the greatest number of humans has proven time and again to be rather utopian and unfeasible.

The painful reality of utopias has been lived to dramatic effect in the context of the global paradigm of modernity—an unending nightmare that has tormented humans in their hundreds of millions. Opposition to this now obvious inhumanity makes us aware of the dynamic produced by the historical search for meaning in *existence* and *coexistence*, that is, the meaning of the *political event*.

Let us recall, in schematic summary form, the factors that we can say with some certainty gave rise to the phenomenon of politics, at least in European history. Throughout ancient Greece there arose, for the first time, the need for a criterion of truth in answer to the question: when is testimony *true* and when is it *false*? It must have been clear to all that the criterion of truth was to be found first in the realm of *existence* and then in the realm of *correct comprehension*. What is true is that which truly *exists*, and what *truly* exists is that which exists always, without change, without decay, without death. The criterion of truth is first and foremost *immortality* (to immortalize).

The Greeks trod the earth and beheld reality, observing and contemplating everything. They sought in the universe of existents something that might be immortal, an indication or measure of immortality. And this empirical investigation provided the Greeks with the assurance that an immortal element did indeed exist in the reality of the universe. But that element was not a something or an entity; it was the *how*, or the *mode*, of reality that was immortal: "the mode of universal governance" (Heraclitus).

This is to say that all of the existents that comprise the universe, every one of them, is ephemeral, decaying, and mortal. However, the *mode* (*logos*) in which every existent exists, along with the *mode* (*logos*) in which existents coexist, is an immortal reality, immutable and everlasting. The only immortal fact in the reality of the universe, experientially and universally verified, is the *logos*-mode in which existents exist and coexist.

Every particular existent (e.g., a lily, a leopard, a cypress tree, an eagle, or a dolphin) exists today, but not tomorrow. Yet the *logos*-mode in which each one of these existents has their ephemeral existence is always the same—immutable, imperishable, and eternal. Moreover, the *logos*-mode in which different existents coexist—the mode of *logos*-possessing harmony, order, and beauty, a mode that makes the universe a *cosmos*-ornament[ii]—is immortal, immutable, and everlasting.

---

i *Alogia*: literally, "non-*logos*."
ii Translator's note: *kosmos-kosmima*. *Kosmos* means "world" in Modern Greek, but in Ancient Greek meant "order" or "decoration/ornament," thus explaining the connection with *kosmima* ("ornament" in Modern Greek), sharing, as they do, a common root.

62 *Materialistic and idealistic utilitarianism*

The Greeks came to the conclusion that everything that can be shared *according to logos* (with relations of harmony and ornamental order) constitutes *truth*, i.e., an immortal reality. Moreover, because they also understood that humans "by nature desire immortality" (Plato), they sought to organize their coexistence (the *relations* that comprise collective life) according to the terms and requirements of truth—the terms of *logos*-possessing harmony and ornamental order. According to the laws of nature, the goal of organized human coexistence is a "communion of need." The Greeks did not reject the communion of need (an act of insanity); they wanted to transform the necessary dictates of instinct into the freedom of *logos*-possessing (harmonious and ordered) relationships, into a contest of freedom.

The product that emerged from this enterprise was called the *polis*, or *political life*. With the eclipse of the Greek perspective and vision, the word *polis* degenerated into something defined by size—human settlements larger than villages and towns.[iii] However, the word's original and primary meaning did not relate to size, but rather to a qualitative enterprise—an organized form of coexistence that no longer aspired merely to be a *communion of need*, but instead transformed it into a *communion of truth*, a contest of freedom.

And truth, the model and goal of the *political* enterprise, was, as indicated above, "the mode of universal governance"—*logos*-possessing (according to *logos*, order, and harmony) relations that comprise the eternal (immortal) ornamental order of the universe. It is difficult, if not impossible, for us today to conceive (if only intellectually) of a goal and practice in life that prioritizes the search for what is true, rather than what is useful. Still, one might venture to argue that the great surprise of ancient Greece (from democracy to architecture, sculpture, and tragedy) is encapsulated in Aristotle's phrase: "to seek for utility everywhere is entirely unsuited to men that are great-souled and free."[iv] Need and utility were not ignored; they simply did not rank among the most important goals. Truth took precedence over utility. Truth came first.

---

iii Translator's note: the Modern Greek meaning of *polis* is "city" in the English sense of the term.
iv Aristotle, *The Politics*, book VIII, 1388b, 2–4.

22 The *Ecclesia* is the aim of politics

The relationship between Hellenism and Christianity has generated plenty of discussion, particularly regarding whether the ancient Greek conception and interpretation of the real and the existent are compatible with the *Ecclesia's* experience and witness. One perspective (not always articulated with sufficient clarity) maintains that the Hellenic *mode* of thought and practice historically prepared the ground, as a form of instruction, for the Greco-Roman world's acceptance of the ecclesial event.

If there is something in the ancient Greek tradition that allows us, perhaps, to characterize that tradition as "a teacher until Christ," as Paul put it in relation to the Mosaic Law in Gal. 3:24, then one might reasonably think that that something is the Greek version of *truth*: truth as unhidden ("un-" plus "hidden"[i]), hence visible, disclosed, and illuminated—not as correct understanding, but as an experience of participating or partaking in immediate knowledge.

The truth of every existent is constituted by the *logos*-mode in which it partakes of existence—this is what constitutes the shape of its otherness, its immortal *kind*. Moreover, knowledge of the *logos*-mode in which it partakes is itself a form of participation (an experiential event)—it is no mere act of intellectual conceptualization. The same goes for the truth of the *cosmos* (the reality of the universe), which is constituted by the *mode-logos* of the relations in which existents coexist. The same also goes for the truth of every human being, which is also realized as a *logos*-mode of existential uniqueness knowable only through the experience of immediate relationship. The Greeks chose (it was a common and paramount need) to direct their collective coexistence towards (in the service of) not simply the "communion of need," but above all the realization of truth—that mode which forms the *logos*-possessing beauty of the cosmos and the active uniqueness of every human being. The Greeks gave the name *polis* and *political life* to the coexistence that constitutes a

---

i Translator's note: a reference to the etymology of the Greek word for "truth" (*alitheia*), written here with a hyphen to highlight its constituent parts: *a-litheia*.

contest for truth, an icon of the *logos*-possessing relations of the universe's ornamental order.

The *Ecclesia's* gospel (good news) is only one step removed from this search for existential truth. The Greeks transcended the version of truth as utility, the reduction of truth to correct understanding. What interested them was *true* existence, an existence free from limitations and necessities. And the *Ecclesia* provided them with the testimony that the first cause of existence and existents is the freedom of love, of ecstatic[ii] *eros*—in this case a loving, self-transcendent *fatherhood*.

The *Ecclesia* thus came to complete ("fulfill," from the verb "to fill," "to complete," "to perfect") the existential aims of the Greek *polis* and *politics*. This testimony, however, prompts the following question: how did this Greek political (communion-centered) *civilization* (mode of life), as well as the civilizational mode of the *Ecclesia* as a contest of loving communion of life and existence, transmute (and when, how, and by whom) into today's radically alienated form? What intervened to identify contemporary *politics*, on the one hand, with the most extreme form of individualistic utilitarianism based on fortified rights, and the Christian *Ecclesia*, on the other, with an equally individualistic and utilitarian religiosity, a mixture of ideological dogmatism and moral cruelty? One possible explanation is the role of Medieval Western Europe: the cosmogonic change in the demographics of the Western part of the Roman Empire, principally between the fourth and sixth centuries AD, that is, its descent into an irreversible primitiveness.

What stages or phases did the *political* and *ecclesial* event pass through in order to arrive at individualistic utilitarianism? The first phase, and most important in terms of its consequences, was ignorance. The barbarian tribes that invaded Western Europe had neither the lived experience nor the linguistic tools to adopt and assimilate the political and ecclesial tradition of the Greco-Roman world. Their conversion to Christianity was not a voluntary decision, the fruit of comparative evaluations or mature personal need. It was mimicry, and mimicry is always skin-deep and superficial. They adopted Christianity as a *religion*, one certainly superior (more advanced) to their own religion, but a religion nonetheless, replete with the typical characteristics of such a phenomenon: infallible and axiomatic principles of orthodox thought, normative and legalistic deontological ethics, and functional models devoid of existential goals.

Even today, the key words that express the ecclesial experience remain lost in translation—they do not refer to the signifieds of their original Greek prototypes and are semantically confused and obscured in the languages and societies of Western Europe. Once translated, words such as "person," "individual,"

---

ii Translator's note: *ek-stasi*, hyphenated to give the etymological sense of standing outside, thus an *eros* that is self-transcendent (that stands outside itself).

The Ecclesia *is the aim of politics* 65

"nature," "essence," "substance," "salvation," "repentance," "theosis," "mystery," "fatherhood," "sanctification," "grace," and numerous others, refer the Westerner (or someone with a Western education) to the realm of *behavior*, not *existence*.

In Greek, for example, the word "nature" (*fysi*) means existence as necessity, while the word "person" (*prosopo*) means existence as freedom. In European languages, "nature" and "essence" mean a common kind, that is, common external (visible) characteristics, and "person" means exactly the same thing as "individual": a single unit among the many sharing the characteristics that constitute a natural kind. The word "salvation" (*sotiria*) in Greek comes from the verb "to save/to be saved" and means whole,[iii] complete, realizing one's full existential potential, while in Western languages it has come to be identified with preservation and assurance, and with the avoidance of evil and threat. "Repentance" (*metanoia*) in Greek means a change of mind, an alteration in the way one thinks or in one's mindset, and therefore in the stance of one's active *relationship* with surrounding reality. In the West, "repentance" means a change of opinion or a change of decision, acceptance of error, or recognition of misconduct.

The words "theosis," "sanctification," and "mystery" are understood in Western Christianity as allegorical expressions, euphemisms, and metaphors. In the Greek ecclesial tradition, these same words are understood literally. The Greek tradition knows (and attests) two *modes* of existence: the mode of the *uncreated* and the mode of the *created*. That tradition also knows the potential inaugurated (and bestowed) by the incarnation of the uncreated—the potential for the created to exist according to the mode of the uncreated's freedom. When this potential is realized, *theosis* and *sanctification* are in view. The *mode* remains a mystery—not in the sense of enigmatic, but in the sense of ineffable. The signifieds of these words can certainly be understood (possessed) conceptually; however, they can only *be known* through experience, in the same way that love, beauty, motherhood, and fatherhood can be known only by experience.

The barbarian tribes that populated post-Roman Europe employed the ecclesial event as a new religion. By adopting the ecclesial event, they transformed it into a religion. The motives and aims that led them to embrace the ecclesial event determined the shape of what they embraced; the ecclesial event was adopted as an alienated individualistic religion. The invaders desired a religion that was superior to their primitive religion, without losing religion altogether.

---

iii Translator's note: *soos*, etymologically connected to the Greek verb *sozo*, "to save," and the Greek noun *sotiria*, "salvation."

As a general rule, humans religionize in the hope of gaining an ontologically ill-defined hope in the afterlife, as well as domesticated conditions of coexistence prior to death, thanks either to awe or fear of the transcendent. Religion is not tied to the level of collective development (civilization) by accident: the religion that produces the most stable conditions of peace and prosperity is regarded as the best.

What does "religionize" mean? It means to accept and to transform certain intellectual constructs that explain the conditions of nature and regulate human behavior into individual beliefs. Fidelity to the letter of the formulation of interpretive principles constitutes a type of meritorious *orthodoxy*. And consistent adherence to a code of behavioral deontology further constitutes (perhaps more so) a type of meritorious *orthopraxy*. Orthodoxy and orthopraxy constitute (with measurable objectivity) requirements for eternal (unending with respect to measurable time) salvation after death.

The barbarian tribes that settled post-Roman Europe became the historical embodiment of the ecclesial event's alienation in the form of an individualistic religion, although they were not responsible for the genesis of this alienation. The potential of religionization attended the *Ecclesia*'s historical path from its first steps—the "Judaisers" of the apostolic period are evidence of this potential. The *Ecclesia* coexisted with its religionized version in the field of history, in the same way that in the gospel parable the wheat coexisted with the weeds in the field (Matt. 13:24–30). And because the stakes are *life* or *abundant life* (John 10:10)—life free from all existential limitations—the desired outcome must always be secured in the face of a struggle with its negation: wheat and weeds always grow together.

23 Augustine is Europe

The recently arrived settlers in the West made a timely discovery in a local writer, Augustine. His work, along with that of his mentor Ambrose of Milan, constitute perhaps history's most prominent examples of weeds that religionized the *Ecclesia*. They paved the way, prior to the barbarian invasion, for the transition of the ecclesial event (and gospel) from the realm of *existence* to the realm of *behavior*—the transition from access to the truth in the realm of *shared experience* to the realm of *individual correct comprehension*. What seems to have emerged from Augustine and Ambrose is not a school or current of individualistic religiosity, but rather something much wider: a new phase in human history—the first truly implemented civilizational paradigm based on the incontestable dynamic of individualism.

These characterizations of Augustine and Ambrose evaluate and judge their historical legacies, not their personal virtues and qualities. They relate to the course and shape of human history, to the criteria that distinguish the *Ecclesia* from the non-*Ecclesia*, to the marked difference between the *Ecclesia* and religion. For those who evaluate positively the individualistic civilization of the post-Roman West (now global) and its extraordinary achievements, Augustine is the admired foundation of this civilization and one of its most significant contributors. However, according to the measure and standards of the *political* contest of the Greeks and the goals of the *ecclesial* event, Augustine is among the most lamentable contributors to a great historical regression.

In the *City of God*, Augustine lay the foundations of a model that transferred the likeness of God from the realm of *existence* to the realm of *behavior*, radically changing in the process the semantic and experiential content of political and ecclesial vocabulary: "virtue" no longer meant a "quality of disposition," but instead individual merit; "faith" was no longer identifiable with trust, but rather individual assumptions and beliefs; "repentance" became remorse, while "law" ceased to demarcate the goals of the political contest, instead becoming a utilitarian end in itself; institutions were no longer generated by common needs, but were the result of decisions based on the logic of collective utility; education no longer constituted a pathway to the joy of relational communion, but became a means of equipping and arming people to demand benefits, and so on and so forth.

The polarity between the realms of *behavior* and *existence* is a useful methodological schema. Consciousness of behavior probably comes first, both in terms of time and need. Instinctive urges are likely delimited for reasons of functionality, with their delimitation giving rise to an awareness of the distinction between "ought" and "ought not," as well as a sense of archetypal vehicles for an authority that can issue prohibitions.

The authoritative source of prohibitions, as well as the joy of permission, emerges in stages of temporally modulated awareness: mother, father, then later teacher, king, and God. The dominant early experience of reality was probably defined by relationships of utility, with the scope of use determining behavior. Relationship as existential experience came later, often originating in pain and sickness, that is, the first consciousness of inadequacy.

There is no doubt that the human being is ruled by lifelong instinctive drives that are individualistic (self-preservation, imposition-domination, pleasure), albeit not completely: "evil [necessity] lies close at hand" (Rom. 7.21);[i] it lies beside,[ii] existing in parallel to the deep desire for *real life*, for loving self-transcendence and self-offering, for the desire of shared existence.

There is, however, also the *natural* potential for humans to form relationships. As a *species* driven by need, the human being survives by virtue of being able to *share need* or divide labor. Yet, relationships, in spite of finding their origin in natural necessity, still offer the *potential* of existential self-transcendence and freedom from the determinism of nature: the miracle of love can blossom from sexual relations; commercial relations can constitute a loving communion of need; relationships with color, sound, and marble can constitute art, in other words, a language of shared truth untainted by expediency. A communion of need (division of labor) should serve ("minister to"[iii]) the *polis* and the *ecclesia*'s struggle to make necessary relationships loving, that is, free from necessity.

It is no coincidence that individualism is connected historically (*causally*) with primitivism (*barbarism*), whereas *relationships* (evidence of self-transcending freedom) are connected to the *communal* event, to "cultivation" (*cultura*) and "civilization" (*civilitas*). As such, today's genuinely global civilizational paradigm constitutes a problem for political thought and comes as something of a surprise in the light of historical experience.

---

i Translator's note: translation taken from the NRSV, square bracket's Yannaras'.
ii Translator's note: *keitai-para*. Yannaras here highlights the etymology of the verb *parakeitai* in Rom. 7:21, which is translated in the NRSV as "lies close at hand."
iii Translator's note: *ypourgei*, the verbal form of the Greek word for "minister" (*ypourgos*), as in "foreign minister" or "minister of education."

Today's paradigm embodies the astonishing fruition of utilitarianism's full potential, whether in relation to the application of science or the organizational functionality of social institutions. It is a case of an extremely consistent and absolute form of individualism, the likes of which history has never seen before. The relevance today of the transference of the *political* and *ecclesial* event from the realm of *existence* to that of *behavior* is not the insight it provides into history (regarding the significance of Ambrose and Augustine, or the invasion and dominance of barbarian tribes in Europe), but its disclosure of a fundamental *crisis of identity* in contemporary Europe.

This crisis of identity is not the product of historical contingencies, but rather of existential choices—the *meaning* (cause and purpose) one chooses to give to existence. This is what determines the goals, the hierarchy of needs, and the priorities that are pursued. The choice between *polis* and *utilitarianism*, *ecclesia* and *religion*, and *creation* and *consumption* are all functions of the existential particularity of human beings, which alone among all existents is able to deny necessity (at least to some extent) and to taste something of existential freedom, if only in the form of nostalgia.

24 Political forms of religious individualism

The transformation of the *Ecclesia* into a religion altered the historical horizon, at least in the societies of Europe and the Middle East. The *Ecclesia* alone proposed a way of understanding (meaning) existence, the cosmos, and history that operated (for several centuries) at the level of illuminating a mode of existence, and not merely at the level of *behavior* and normative deontology. The *Ecclesia* spoke of life and abundant life, never of individual achievements of virtue warranting reward, nor feats of individual self-control.

Accepting that the ecclesial event became a religion offends rational thought (the logic of efficacy). Millions of people throughout the centuries have passed through life and then departed in the absolute confidence that they were Christians, while being oblivious to the reality of the *Ecclesia*. This is, of course, exactly what happens in relation to love or true art of every kind, and the same could happen in relation to friendship or motherhood and fatherhood. The vast majority of people are probably oblivious to, nor ever taste, the miracle of loving self-transcendence and self-offering. Nevertheless, the overwhelming odds of failure do not prevent love, art, friendship, motherhood, and fatherhood from being existential possibilities open to all in perpetuity. They are possible for all, albeit not attainable by all, nor attainable collectively.

One reading of historical developments is to identify instinctive individualism as the origin or kernel of the *Ecclesia's* transformation into a religion, that is, the human urge for *self-preservation* and the driving need for *individual salvation*, whereby the ego finds assurance in the proven certainty of an immortality purchased in exchange for measurable good works, moral self-control, and obedience to legal ordinances.

How is religious individualism given political form? Somebody must certify or evaluate individual achievements in order for the ego's fortification to be objectively assured. That role is bestowed upon the *clergy* (bishops and priests), thus circumventing the categorical and fundamental distinction between *teacher* and *father* made by Paul—the teacher's task concerns *behavior*, the father's role concerns *existence*. In the context of religionization, everything is transferred to, and understood at, the level of behavior, so that

DOI: 10.4324/9781003410867-25

behavior can be monitored and assessed, much like we measure the size of an object. Thus, *fatherhood* gets conceived metaphorically and iconologically, instead of being understood literally. The fatherhood exercised by bishops or priests gets described as "spiritual," so that it might be reified as a psychological process.

Once the *ecclesial event* is misconstrued as a work of behavioral *instruction*, *orthodoxy* and *orthopraxy* become the two obvious bases (criteria) upon which the work can be individually appropriated. Members of the *Ecclesia* are obliged to possess the correct beliefs and to behave correctly, while the *clergy* teach and monitor beliefs and behavior to ensure that they are correct. The clergy are not held accountable by either a sense of communal responsibility or the experience of fatherhood, that is, by the institution of the episcopal *synod*. In the religionized *Ecclesia*, the clergy are accountable to the most prestigious bishop, one whose primacy is established according to criteria completely at odds with those of the *Ecclesia*, which is to say, according to historical titles and sacral privileges.

The logic of appointing a supreme power and authority in the religionized ecclesia is immature and reflects the developmental level of Europe's barbarian settlers in the post-Roman period. The logic says that Christ was the founder of the Christian religion, just like Buddha was the founder of Buddhism, Zoroaster of Zoroastrianism, and Muhammad of Islam. Christ entrusted his work to his disciples and apostles. Who among Christ's disciples was in charge? Who was the leader? It is argued from the texts of Holy Scriptures (albeit not uniformly) that it was Peter. Peter visited Rome and was martyred there. Hence, he is assumed to be the first bishop of Rome, even if this is a perversion of historical truth. Every bishop of Rome is a successor to the first bishop of Rome, the apostle Peter. Peter was first among apostles, and therefore all his successors are first among bishops in the world. As the first, he can be regarded as "Christ's representative" (*vicarius Christi*), possessing absolute authority over the earth.

25 The *Ecclesia's* alienation in confessionalism

The excessive and arbitrary exercise of the bishop-Pope of Rome's authority fertilized the ground (in complete consistency with the "physiology" of history) for the revolutionary explosion of "Protestantism" (Protestantismus). Protestantism did not reject the totalitarian idea of subjection to an infallible authority. Rather, it rejected the personification of that authority, transferring infallibility to the authority of the "Holy Scriptures" (*Sola Scriptura*). In this way, the authoritative power of reified truth became accessible to any clever, capable, or charismatic interpreter of the Holy Scriptures—Protestant truth splintered into as many versions as there were talented interpreters.

Christian truth ceased to be an *event*, the shared achievement or gift of participating in the realization of the gospel (good news). It ceased to be an *Ecclesia*, a bond of communal relations, instead becoming a *confession*: the organized coordination of individual assumptions, beliefs, and intellectual and volitional certainties. The transfer of papal infallibility to individual interpretive versions of the inspired truth of Holy Scripture generated the unprecedented phenomenon of ideology.

In speaking of the religionization of the *Ecclesia*, we are not pointing to a misunderstanding or misuse of the ecclesial event, but to its alienation, distortion, transformation, and transmutation. The *Ecclesia* became something alien, foreign, different to what it *is*, in a rejection, adulteration, or perversion of its truth. The *Ecclesia* is concerned with *existence*, the *mode* of existence, a *communion* of existence, while religion is concerned with individual metaphysical *beliefs* and an individual mode of *behavior*, conduct, and morality.

The realm of *existence* and the realm of *belief* and *behavior* are completely different. No existent—not even the *logos*-possessing human—can interfere with the terms (given facts) of its existence. Existents do not choose to exist or *how* they exist. Humans, for example, cannot alter their height, sex, physique, or intellectual ability. Nor do they choose their parents, mother tongue, society, race, culture, or era in which they happen to live. The *logos*-possessing human being does not verify its defining existential difference purely on the basis of the function of its intellect (the function of understanding), but primarily through *experience*, which is to say, through its participation in *relational*

DOI: 10.4324/9781003410867-26

events that constitute its evolving existence.[i] The human being does not come to know maternal care, love, or the otherness of artistic creation, for example, by understanding information. It does so by participating in *relationships* with the reality in which it is embedded.

Humans can, on the other hand, intervene decisively in the realm of behavior, setting its terms and boundaries, goals and pursuits, and incentives and presuppositions. Humans can impose, either by consensus or the power of majority, principles of law, regulations, moral rules, and institutions of order and correction. Human *intelligence* is the original source of such interventions, which is to say, understanding human needs (ascertaining, as well as foreseeing them), prioritizing those needs, and identifying (clarifying) how to satisfy them. Once the utility, instrumentality, and efficacy of human actions and activity, along with their intentions, have been correctly understood, the accuracy of that understanding is codified and functions as a standard for evaluating behavior (the codification is of course conventional and instrumental, as individual judgments of accuracy never converge absolutely).

Birth and death, growth and decline, wholeness and privation, strength and weakness, maturity and immaturity, and health and sickness are examples of indicative categories (linguistic signifiers) that refer to the *existential* event, or which define that event. Examples of indicative categories (linguistic signifiers) that refer to the realm of *behavior* are correct and mistaken, right and wrong, lawful and unlawful, moral and immoral, and ought and ought not.

Comprehension of the terminology alone suffices to demonstrate (illuminate) the crucial difference between these two realms. Conditions in the *existential* realm occur and function despite human will (freedom)—the human being is only able to influence indirectly (with "practice"[ii] and concerted effort) some of the factors that govern its existential identity, such as diet and exercise as a means of controlling one's physical state, or suitable teaching as a means of instilling kindness and modesty. However, with these examples we have already slipped into the realm of *behavior*. Behavior certainly influences the function of the existential event in the same way that certain existential functions influence behavior. The influence is reciprocal, albeit not decisive or deterministic.

The brief classification above illuminates, or clarifies, two related facts of common experience. It makes sense, although it is not necessary, that the demand for individual (egoistic) *meritorious reward* should only arise in the realm of behavior. It would obviously be nonsensical for such a demand to emerge in the existential realm. There is a certain logic to taking pride in behavioral virtues, like self-control, reliability, kindness, and honesty. There is, however, no logic whatsoever to boasting of anything such as acuity, physical beauty, sharp eyesight, a beautiful voice, or anything similar—this would be comical.

---

i Translator's note: *to gignesthai tis yparxis tou*, literally "the becoming of its existence."
ii Translator's note: *ascesis*.

26 A Trinitarian archetype of politics

Relationship is the crucial term for verifying and apprehending the *ecclesial* event, as distinct from *religion*, and the *political* (*polis*) event, as distinct from coexistence as domination.

In both the Greek *political* (*polis*) tradition and the Christian *Eclessia*, the word "relationship" refers to the realm of existence, and only by misapplication (by conflation) to the realm of behavior. According to the ancient Greeks, the *logos*-possessing *relations* of existents (according to *logos*, order, and harmony) were a necessary condition for their existence. Existents exist *because* they coexist *according to logos*, the *logos*-possessing *mode* in which they coexist, that is, "the mode of universal governance."

This means that the *mode* of *logos*-possessing relations for the totality of existents (the *cosmos* in its entirety) is the mode of *being*. Relations possessing *logos* (order, harmony, ornamentality) are a precondition of being, which is to say, a *mode* of immortality. This truth—the disclosure of the immortal *logos*-possessing ornamental order—is decisively and inexplicably given. It is a necessity that determines every aspect of existence, a rigid determinism binding even the gods (their existence and role). The remarkable Greek conception of truth (unhidden) as the disclosure of *immortality*—an immortal *mode* or *way* of the universe's ornamental order—was accompanied by the logically obligatory acceptance of an uninterpretable (deterministic) given necessity. In the Greek worldview, there was no room for existential freedom, for an unpredetermined existence, for existential otherness. The *logikotita*[i] of everything was inexplicably given.

Still, identifying truth as immortality with the *logos*-possessing ornamental order of *relations*, and making this the exclusive goal of knowledge, generated the historical reality of the Greek *polis*, the "common contest" of *political* life and *democracy*, the fruits of the unique Greek "desire for immortality," the desire to give priority to what is *true* over what is *useful*. Moreover, active consciousness of the determinism and necessity of the *logos*-mode that

---

i Translator's note: *logikotita*, literally "*logos*-ness."

DOI: 10.4324/9781003410867-27

universally governs the existential event gave birth to Greek *tragedy*, the first and most significant memorialization of the longing for existential freedom in human literature.

The gospel (good news) and witness of the Christian *Ecclesia*, as we have come to know it, specifically addressed the ontological impasse created by the determinism and necessity that governs, primordially and conclusively, the existential event, as interpreted by the Greeks. In ecclesial experience, the *logikotita* (*logos*-ness) of relations that constitutes existence and the coexistence of existents is not given, that is, uninterpretable necessity, but rather the disclosure-*logos* of an unlimited freedom. We have already analyzed in these pages the foundational source of ecclesial distinctiveness. The first cause of existence and existents is, according to ecclesial experience, the freedom of mutual love, a freedom that exists because it wills to exist, and wills to exist because it loves.

Human language (and intellect) attempts to signify this reality that lies beyond the boundaries of the created world (the limits of our language) by characterizing the first cause of existence and existents not as God, which is bound to exist by the necessities of a prescribed divine *essence*, but as Father. The word "Father" denotes a *logos*-possessing existence that "instantiates"[ii] (constitutes or gives reality to) an *ecstatic*[iii] (loving) *mode* of existence by "begetting" and "sending forth" those who receive and freely reciprocate the love of that existence, without any separation or division in their shared *mode* of existence, that is, the *essence* of this Trinitarian existential event.

According to our linguistic code, the concept or image of *fatherhood* denotes a *hypostatic* active freedom, not of individual will, but of shared mutual love. The freedom of individual will is limited to unhindered individual choice and preference, while the freedom of shared mutual love constitutes a *mode* of existence free from all determinism and necessity.

The *Father* exists because he "begets" the *Son* and "sends forth" the *Spirit*, "timelessly and lovingly." The Father does not exist as a *hypostatic* monad temporally or qualitatively prior to his begetting and sending forth. Rather, he exists (*he is*) *because* "he begets" and "sends forth" *lovingly* (in perfect freedom). He exists as freedom, that is, as love, in the begetting and the sending forth. The first cause of existence—its *mode* of existence, its *essence*, its definition—is not something given, but rather a timeless (with no *before* or *after*) and free realization of love—a *hypostatic* (not simply volitional) realization (begetting and sending forth). "God *is* love" (1 John 4:16); the first cause of existence is absolute freedom.

---

ii Translator's note: *ypostasiazei*, literally "*hypostasizes*."
iii Translator's note: *ek-statiko*. The Greek word for "ecstatic," hyphenated to give the etymological sense of "standing outside," i.e., self-transcendent.

27 Comprehension is not knowledge

The image (perspective) that a human society has of the reality of the universe, the interpretation it chooses and adopts for the origin and function of the whole cosmos, appears to reflect its own composition and function. The monotheistic version of the cause and function of the universe points directly to forms of authority, such as kingship, monarchy, and despotism. Polytheism seems to echo forms of authority that are pyramidal and polymerous. An agnosticism that is consistent with respect to the metaphysical purpose of reality, or that naively accepts chance as the first cause of existence, leads to the necessity of organizing human coexistence and cohabitation on the basis of a collective treaty-contract, the terms of which bind members of the collective to self-restraints that are fundamentally useful.

In the cases of ancient Greek *democracy* and the Christian *Ecclesia* (the political form of the Greco-Roman world), our sources testify in a way that leaves no room for interpretive doubt: the originating source of both political forms was the common and experientially shared will, desire, and goal for the organization and function of collective life to realize the *mode* of *truth*: the immortal and immutable *mode of universal governance* (the *logos*-possessing ornamental order and harmony) or the *mode* of loving freedom (the Trinitarian interpenetration[i] of existence), which is to say, the identification of existence with the freedom of self-transcending self-determination.

Today, we lack the relevant experiential apperceptions to apprehend the ancient Greek and ecclesial version of politics (and authority)—*comprehending* signifiers does not lead to *knowledge* of their signifieds. We are fixed in the habit (automatic reflex) of conceiving reality as an individual entity, not a developing otherness, nor the freedom of relationship, nor an event self-determined by a freedom that is not subject to predetermined constants. We self-evidently assume that existence is prior to act (relations).

It is not theoretical differences that are at issue here, but incompatible and incommensurate *modes* of thought and action—radically antithetical and

---

i Translator's note: *aplliloperichoresi*, literally "inter-perichoresis."

DOI: 10.4324/9781003410867-28

mutually exclusive *aims* of existence and life. The ancient Greek and ecclesial version of politics and authority is separated from the medieval Western European and contemporary globalized version by an unbridgeable chasm that opposes *truth* to *utility*—truth, as the shared aim of existential freedom, versus utility, as individual-centered security and pleasure.

The difference between *communion-centered* priorities and *individual-centered* priorities divides human history in two. Individual-centered priorities are chronologically and developmentally prior, and clearly reflect primitivism, subjection to instinct, and protection of the ego. Communion-centered priorities are born once the human being is possessed by a love of immortality, having tasted the indestructible beauty of *logos*-possessing "harmony and ornamental order"—"longing for it and rushing after it."[ii]

It is extremely difficult today, if not impossible, to even comprehend that existential truth as immortality might be a superior need to utilitarian individual protection. We lack the lived experience to know that *comprehending* signifiers does not bring about *knowledge* of their signifieds. We find it very difficult to approach a reality that identifies *existence* with *communion*. We presuppose that existence is given and that relational communion is an act. We therefore also find it very difficult to understand the first cause of existence as *love*, rather than atomicity (a God), which is to say as an existential event of *relationship*, as fatherhood, sonship, and the father's *spirit*. Correspondingly, it is very difficult for us to identify *democracy* with the shared contest for truth and communion rather than the protection of individual rights in accordance with a contract.

September 2018

---

ii Plato, *The Republic*, Book IV, 439b.

Bibliography

Aristotle. *The Eudemian Ethics*. Translated and revised by H. Rackham. Cambridge, MA: Harvard University Press, 1952.
———. *Metaphysics*. Translated by Hugh Tredennick. London: William Heinemann, 1933.
———. *The Nicomachean Ethics*. Translated by H. Rackham. Cambridge, MA: Harvard University Press, 1934.
———. *Physics*. Translated and revised by Philip H. Wicksteed and Francis M. Cornford. London: William Heinemann, 1957.
———. *Poetics*. Translated and with a commentary by George Whalley. Montreal: McGill-Queen's University Press, 1997.
———. *Politics*. Translated by H. Rackham. Cambridge, MA: Harvard University Press, 1944.
Böckenförde, Ernst Wolfgang. *Die Entstehung des Staates als Vorgang der Säkularisation*. Stuttgart: Kolhammer Verlag, 1967.
Diels, Hermann, and Walther Kranz, eds. *Die Fragmente der Vorsokratiker*. Berlin: Weidmannsche Verlagabuchhandlung, 1952.
Heraclitus. *Fragments: A Text and Translation with a Commentary by T.M. Robinson*. Toronto: University of Toronto Press, 1987.
Kalaitzidis, Pantelis. "New Trends in Greek Orthodox Theology: Challenges in the Movement towards a Genuine Renewal and Christian Unity." *Scottish Journal of Theology* 67, no. 2 (2014): 127–64.
Kastoriadis, Cornelius. *Ancient Greek Democracy and Its Significance for Us Today*. Athens: Ypsilon, 1999.
Milbank, John, and Adrian Pabst. *The Politics of Virtue: Post-Liberalism and the Human Future*. London: Rowman & Littlefield, 2016.
Plato. *Cratylus*. Translated by H.N. Fowler. Cambridge, MA: Harvard University Press, 1939.
———. *Gorgias*. Translated and revised by W.R.M. Lamb. London: William Heinemann, 1932.
———. *Laws*. Translated and revised by W.R.M. Lamb. London: William Heinemann, 1939.
———. *Protagoras*. Translated and revised by W.R.M. Lamb. London: William Heinemann, 1937.
———. *Republic Books 1–5*. Edited and translated by Chris Emlyn-Jones and William Preddy. Cambridge, MA: Harvard University Press, 2013.

Pseudo-Dionysius. "The Divine Names." In *Pseudo-Dionysius: The Complete Works*. Translated by Colm Luibheid. New York: Paulist Press, 1987.

Sakellariou, Michail. *Athenian Democracy*. Heraklion: Crete University Press, 1999.

Williams, Rowan. "The Theology of Personhood: A Study of the Thought of Christos Yannaras." *Sobornost* 6 (1972): 415–30.

Yannaras, Christos. *The Effable and the Ineffable: The Linguistic Boundaries of Metaphysical Realism*. Translated by Jonathan Cole, edited and with an introduction by Andreas Andreopoulos. Winchester: Winchester University Press, 2021.

———. *Finis Graeciae*. Thessaloniki: Ianos, 2014.

———. *The Inhumanity of Right*. Translated by Norman Russell. Cambridge: James Clarke & Co, 2021.

———. *The Schism in Philosophy: The Hellenic Perspective and Its Western Reversal*. Translated by Norman Russell. Brookline, MA: Holy Cross Orthodox Press, 2015.

———. "A Note on Political Theology." Translated by Peter Tsichlis. *St Vladimir's Theological Quarterly* 27, no. 1 (1983): 53–6.

———. *Person and Eros*. Translated by Norman Russell. Brookline, MA: Holy Cross Orthodox Press, 2008.

———. *Ἀντιπαλεύοντας τὸ πολιτικὸ τίποτα* [*Resisting Political Nihilism*]. Thessaloniki: Ianos, 2019.

———. *Ἀντιστάσεις στὴν ἀλλοτρίωση* [*Resisting Alienation*] 2nd ed. Athens: Ikaros, 2008.

———. *Ἀντιχάρισμα στὸν Νίτσε* [*Homage to Nietzsche*]. Athens: Ikaros, 2020.

———. *Ἡ Ἀριστερὰ ὡς Δεξιὰ—Ἡ Δεξιὰ ὡς παντομίμα* [*The Left as Right—The Right as Pantomime*] 2nd ed. Athens: Patakis, 2001.

———. *Ἀφελληνισμοῦ παρεπόμενα* [*The Consequences of De-Hellenization*] 2nd ed. Athens: Kaktos, 2005.

———. *Εἰς μικρὸν γενναῖοι—Ὁδηγίες χρήσεως* [*A Guide to Being Brave Against the Odds*]. Athens: Patakis, 2003.

———. *Ἑλλαδικὰ προτελεύτια* [*The End of the Greek State*] 2nd ed. Athens: Kastaniotis, 1992.

———. *Ἑλληνοκεντρικὸς ἐκσυγχρονισμός* [*Greek-Centric Modernization*]. Thessaloniki: Ianos, 2018.

———. *Ἑλληνικὴ ἑτοιμότητα γιὰ τὴν εὐρωπαϊκὴ ἑνοποίηση* [*Is Greece Ready for Union with Europe?*]. Athens: Livanis, 2000.

———. *Ἡ ἑλληνικότητα ὡς ποιότητα καὶ ὡς ντροπή* [*Greek Identity as Quality and Shame*]. Thessaloniki: Ianos, 2014.

———. *Ἑλληνότροπος πολιτική* [*The Greek Style of Politics*]. Athens: Ikaros, 1996.

———. *Ἐνθάδε—Ἐπέκεινα (ἀπόπειρες ὀντολογικῆς ἑρμηνευτικῆς)* [*Here and Beyond (An Attempt at Ontological Interpretation)*]. Athens: Ikaros, 2016.

———. *Ἔπαινος ψήφου τιμωρητικῆς* [*In Praise of a Protest Vote*] 2nd ed. Thessaloniki: Ianos, 2008.

———. *Ἰχνηλασία νοήματος* [*Outline of Meaning*]. Athens: Livanis, 1998.

———. *Τὰ καθ' ἑαυτὸν* [*Memoires*] 4th ed. Athens: Ikaros, 2005.

———. *Κατὰ κεφαλὴν καλλιέργεια* [*Per Capita Cultivation*] 2nd ed. Thessaloniki: Ianos, 2011.

———. *Ἡ κατάρρευση τοῦ πολιτικοῦ συστήματος στὴν Ἑλλάδα σήμερα* [*The Collapse of the Political System in Greece Today*] 2nd ed. Thessaloniki: Ianos, 2010.

———. *Καταφύγιο Ἰδεῶν* [*Refuge of Ideas*] 8th ed. Athens: Ikaros, 2011.

80 Bibliography

―――. *Τὸ κενὸ στὴν τρέχουσα πολιτικὴ* [*The Void in Contemporary Politics*] 4th ed. Athens: Ikaros, 2010.

―――. *Κεφάλαια Πολιτικῆς Θεολογίας* [*Chapters in Political Theology*] 3rd ed. Athens: Grigoris, 1973.

―――. *Κοινωνιοκεντρικὴ Πολιτική: Κριτήρια* [*Criteria for a Communion-Centered Politics*]. Athens: Estias, 2007.

―――. *Κομματοκρατία* [*Rule by Parties*] 3rd ed. Athens: Patakis, 2004.

―――. *Ἡ κρίση τῆς προφητείας* [*Prophetic Judgment*] 4th ed. Athens: Ikaros, 2010.

―――. *Κριτικὲς παρεμβάσεις* [*Critical Interventions*] 4th ed. Athens: Domos, 1993.

―――. *Ἡ λογικὴ ἀρχίζει μὲ τὸν ἔρωτα* [*Logic Begins with Love*] 2nd ed. Athens: Ikaros, 2007.

―――. *Μαχόμενη ἀνελπιστία* [*Fighting the Unexpected*] 2nd ed. Athens: Estias, 2005.

―――. *Νὰ ἐπαναστατήσει ἡ ἀξιοπρέπεια* [*Self-Respect Demands Revolt*]. Thessaloniki: Ianos, 2011.

―――. *Ἡ Νεοελληνικὴ Ταυτότητα* [*Neo-Hellenic Identity*] 4th ed. Athens: Grigoris, 2001.

―――. *Ὀντολογία τοῦ προσώπου (προσωποκεντρικὴ ὀντολογία)* [*An Ontology of Personhood (A Person-Centered Ontology)*]. Athens: Ikaros, 2016.

―――. *Ὀρθὸς λόγος καὶ κοινωνικὴ πρακτική* [*Rationalism and Social Practice*]. Athens: Domos, 1984.

―――. *Παιδεία καὶ γλώσσα* [*Education and Language*] 5th ed. Athens: Patakis, 2003.

―――. *Ἡ παρακμὴ ὡς πρόκληση* [*Decline as Provocation*]. Athens: Livanis, 2000.

―――. *Ἡ πολιτικὴ γονιμότητα τῆς ὀργῆς* [*The Fertile Politics of Anger*]. Thessaloniki: Ianos, 2011.

―――. *Πολιτικὴ χρονογραφία 1: Χώρα ὑποχείρια παιγνίου* [*Political Chronicles Part 1: A Country That Is a Pawn in a Game*]. Athens: Kastaniotis, 1994.

―――. *Πολιτικὴ χρονογραφία 2: Ἀπερισκέπτως αὐτόχειρες* [*Political Chronicles Part 2: Rushing to Suicide*]. Athens: Kastaniotis, 1994.

―――. *Πολιτικὴ χρονογραφία 3: Κύκλος φαύλος στροβιλώδης* [*Political Chronicles Part 3: A Turbulent Vicious Circle*]. Athens: Kastaniotis, 1994.

―――. *Τὸ πολιτικὸ ζητούμενο στὴν Ἑλλάδα σήμερα* [*The Political Challenge in Greece Today*] 2nd ed. Thessaloniki: Ianos, 2010.

―――. *Πολιτισμός, τὸ κεντρικὸ πρόβλημα τῆς πολιτικῆς* [*Culture: The Central Problem of Politics*] 2nd ed. Athens: Kaktos, 2005.

―――. *Τὸ πραγματικὸ καὶ τὸ φαντασιῶδες στὴν Πολιτικὴ Οἰκονομία* [*Reality and Illusion in Political Economy*]. Athens: Domos, 2006.

―――. *Τὸ πρόβλημά μας εἶναι πολιτικό, ὄχι οἰκονομικὸ* [*Our Problem Is Political, Not Economic*]. Thessaloniki: Ianos, 2013.

―――. *Τὸ προνόμιο τῆς ἀπελπισίας* [*The Prerogative of Despair*] 2nd ed. Athens: Grigoris, 1973.

―――. *Προφορικὴ ἀμεσότητα* [*Verbal Immanence*] 2nd ed. Thessaloniki: Ianos, 2003.

―――. *Πτώση, Κρίση, Κόλαση ἢ δικανικὴ ὑπονόμευση τῆς ὀντολογίας* [*Fall, Judgment and Hell, Or the Way that Legalistic Thinking Undermines Ontology*]. Athens: Ikaros, 2017.

―――. *Τὴν ἀλήθεια κατάματα* [*Staring Truth in the Face*]. Thessaloniki: Ianos, 2017.

―――. *Τόπος τοῦ ἀνοίκειου τρόπου* [*In an Unfamiliar Mode*]. Thessaloniki: Ianos, 2015.

Index

Ambrose of Milan 67, 69
Anselm of Canterbury 55
Aquinas, Thomas 55
Areopagite 6
Aristotle 6, 56, 58, 62
Augustine viii, 50, 67, 69
authority 10, 16, 19, 21–6, 28–9, 36, 43, 50–2, 54–5, 57–8, 68, 71–2, 76–7; absolute 50, 52, 71; exercise of 23, 26, 43, 51; infallible 59, 72; metaphysical 16, 23, 51, 53; papal 53; political 9, 23–4, 27; and religion 17; religious 23; Roman 41; Rome's 72; temporal 27; totalitarian 51; transcendent 15, 25

Bakunin, Mikhail 53
barbarian 23–6, 48, 50, 58, 64, 66–7, 69, 71
Böckenförde, Wolfgang 23, 25–6, 51
Bonhoeffer, Dietrich viii
Byzantium 3, 10, 34

Calvin, John 53
Catholic 4
Charlemagne 24
Christianity vii–viii, 5, 10–11, 25–6, 41, 48, 50, 53, 57–8, 63–5
church vii–viii, 4, 11, 49, 58
civilization vii, 4, 12, 33, 46, 48, 57, 64, 66–8
communion vii, 10–11, 19–20, 26, 31–4, 36, 46, 53–4, 59, 77; -centered 11, 55, 59, 64, 77; *ecclesial* 47; of existence 72; of experience 34, 55; of life 64; of love 43; of need 11, 19, 28, 32, 40–1, 44, 62–3, 68; participatory 32; political 33; relational 11, 59, 68, 77; of truth 10, 28, 44, 62
convention 23, 36, 55, 58–9

democracy 5, 9, 11, 16, 24, 33–4, 43–7, 60, 62, 74, 76–7
Democritus 30
deontology 16, 23, 66

ecclesia 9–11, 26, 40–3, 45, 48–50, 59–60, 63–4, 66–7, 69, 70–2, 75–6

freedom vii, 8, 10, 13, 15, 37–8, 41–3, 47, 53, 55–6, 59, 62, 65, 68, 73, 75–6; from all necessity 42; contest of 62; existence as 42, 47, 65; existential 42, 44, 69, 74–5; of love 64; and love vii; loving 10, 76; mode of 41; necessity and 15; of relationship 42, 76; religious 51
Freud, Sigmund 20, 53

God 9–10, 15, 18, 21, 25–6, 28, 41–2, 49–50, 52–3, 67–8, 75, 77
gods 13–14, 22, 74

Heidegger, Martin 6
Hellenism 9, 57–8, 63
Heraclitus 10, 18, 27–8, 30, 34, 41, 61
Hermes 13

82 Index

ideology viii, 3, 11, 45, 47, 52–3, 72
immortality 29, 32, 35, 40, 44, 61–2, 70, 74
individualism vii, 3, 11–12, 14, 16, 41, 49, 57, 59–60, 67–70

Lacan, Jacques 6
law/s vii, 7, 11, 15, 21, 45, 62, 67, 73; divine 8, 15; Hebrew 9; Mosaic 21, 28, 63
leitourgima 10, 19–21
Lenin, Vladimir 53
logikotita 17, 36, 38, 74–5
logos 9–10, 18, 27, 29–31, 33–4, 41–2, 49, 61–2, 75; in- 22, 40; according to 16, 19, 22, 27, 32–3, 35, 41, 62, 74; -mode 17–18, 22, 61, 63–4, 74; non- 22; -possessing 9, 18–19, 22, 30, 32–3, 36, 38, 40–1, 43, 61–4, 72, 74–7; -relations 18
love vii, 10, 15, 41–3, 49, 54, 59–60, 64–5, 68, 70, 73, 75, 77
Luther, Martin 53

Mao Zedong 53
Marx, Karl 53
Maximus the Confessor 6
metaphysics 6, 9, 16, 21, 23, 25, 28, 35–6, 50
mode 5, 8, 10–11, 13–14, 16, 18, 26–9, 33, 37, 39–40, 43–8, 59, 61, 63–5, 70, 74–6; of behavior 72; of coexistence 32, 35, 46; of createdness 59; of existence 10–11, 13, 16, 27, 29, 43, 48–9, 59, 72, 75; of freedom 41; Hellenic 63; of immortality 32, 35, 74; of life 33, 46, 64; *logos*- 17–18, 61, 63, 74; of loving freedom 76; of rational order 13; of relations 22, 33; of truth 27, 32–3, 44, 76; of universal governance 22, 27, 40–1, 44, 61–2, 74, 76; by which the universe is governed 35
modernity viii, 54, 56–7, 61
monarchy 5, 22, 43, 76

necessity 8–10, 15, 22, 32–4, 36–7, 41–6, 49, 59, 65, 68–9, 74–6

need vii, 8, 10, 13–14, 20, 22–4, 28, 32–3, 36, 40–2, 50–3, 57, 61–4, 68–70, 73, 77; collective 27; common 20, 22, 32, 44, 46, 67; communion of 11, 19, 28, 33, 40, 44, 62–3, 68; human 22, 73; individual 10, 14, 42; natural 32; shared 10, 35, 46, 68; sharing of 16, 33, 35; utilitarian 52
Newman, John Henry viii

ontological vii, 1, 7, 11–12, 44–6, 66, 75
order 16, 26–7, 33–4, 38, 43, 49, 61–2, 73–4, 76; good 21–2, 41; harmony and 19, 32, 34; ornamental 16, 19, 22, 35, 62, 64, 74, 77; political 27; rational 13; of relations 9; of things 25, 57–8
ornamentality 19, 22, 32, 41, 43, 74
Orthodox 2–6, 9, 11

Plato 13, 44, 62
polytheism 76
Pope 26–7, 52, 72
potential 9, 11, 15, 38–9, 50, 59, 65–6, 68–9
Protagoras 13
Protestant 4–5, 52, 72

ratio 23, 25
religion vii, 3, 11–12, 16–17, 24, 26–7, 48–52, 64–7, 69–71, 74
religionization 48, 66, 70, 72
Roman Empire 11, 23, 41, 57, 64

salvation 11, 24, 27, 49, 50, 57, 60, 65–6, 70
Sartre, John-Paul 6
secularization 23, 27, 54
signifieds 44, 64, 76–7
signifiers 8, 31, 45, 73, 76–7
Smith, Adam 53

totalitarianism 12, 50, 52–3
Trinitarian 10, 42–3, 74–6
truth vii, 8, 10–11, 15, 21–2, 28, 30, 32–5, 41–4, 47–8, 50, 52–3, 55, 57–9, 62–4, 67, 71–2, 74, 77; according to 27, 29, 40, 45–6, 49; communion of 10, 28, 44, 62;

contest for 33, 63, 77; criterion of 28–31, 33, 61; ecclesial 50; of existence 12; existential 46, 63, 77; mode of 32, 44, 76; political 7; shared 35, 68

unhidden 8, 10, 29–30, 43–4, 55, 58, 63, 74

utilitarianism 16, 23–4, 27, 35, 43, 47, 60, 64, 69

Williams, Rowan 6
Wittgenstein, Ludwig 6

Zeus 13
Zwingli, Huldrych 53

Taylor & Francis eBooks

www.taylorfrancis.com

A single destination for eBooks from Taylor & Francis with increased functionality and an improved user experience to meet the needs of our customers.

90,000+ eBooks of award-winning academic content in Humanities, Social Science, Science, Technology, Engineering, and Medical written by a global network of editors and authors.

TAYLOR & FRANCIS EBOOKS OFFERS:

- A streamlined experience for our library customers
- A single point of discovery for all of our eBook content
- Improved search and discovery of content at both book and chapter level

REQUEST A FREE TRIAL
support@taylorfrancis.com